Be Funny

Be Funny

A Practical Guide to Everyday Humor

Peter White

*For Suzanne, my mother, and my father –
all whose patience and support
made this possible.*

Table of Contents

Introduction

The best thing I ever did in my life was deciding to become funny. And it **was** a decision.

Being funny does more than just make people laugh, it makes people like you. It establishes a connection that goes beyond the surface level. It sounds cheesy, but in order for you to make someone laugh on a consistent basis, you have to understand them. You have to know how their mind works. And that means a lot to a person. It shows that you understand them, which makes them feel less alone. It's a primal connection that draws people together.

Being able to build those connections can drastically improve your life. Studies have shown that funny people are generally perceived as:

- More Intelligent
- More confident
- More Desirable
- More Empathetic
- More Successful

Being funny is one of the best short cuts for improving your social life. Realistically, a better short cut is to be super hot or incredibly rich, but it's a lot easier to get funny than it is to become a billionaire or a supermodel. Becoming funny is like getting in shape: anyone can do it, but it takes a lot of work. You need to train your brain to think in a funny way. This book will show you the method, but it's up to you to put in the work.

I wasn't naturally funny. In fact, before I was a stand up comedian, I was an electrical engineer, which is about as funny as dirt. As a kid I loved math and dinosaurs and dreamed of being a scientist. I was a nerd through and through. If I wasn't me, I'd have bullied me. Sure, I got great grades and won nerd contests in computers, but I had very few friends. I didn't mind being a loner, until puberty hit, and my priorities changed.

Suddenly dinosaurs seemed quite a bit less interesting than girls, though just as unattainable. Teachers made it seem as though good grades were the way to a good life, but I couldn't help but notice that most of the kids with lower grades were having a lot more fun.

It came to a head at my first junior high dance. I didn't know how to dance, and I was too scared to talk to people, so I spent the evening hovering on the edge of circles and pretending I was a part of them. I'd stick around until someone stared at me too long, then I'd zip off to another circle.

That was all well and good while Smash Mouth and Cotton Eye Joe were playing, but as we got later in the night the slow songs started sneaking in. All around me, people started coupling off. I panicked. Not knowing what to do, I ducked to the bathroom, planning to ride out All-4-One's *I Swear* at the urinal. Turns out 3:43 is a long time to fake pee, so I had some time to take in my surroundings. As I was standing there, not peeing, I noticed a small figure next to me. It was a fellow loser, from the grade above me. I recognized him but he didn't know me - because even losers don't notice younger losers. After about 30 seconds, it became obvious that he wasn't peeing either. We were both just standing there hiding from the world. Eventually he looked at me, and he said in a timid voice: "you too?"

In that moment I made a declaration to myself: this is not how you're going to live. I didn't know how, but I was not going to live my whole life hiding at the urinal.

Figuring it Out

At some point in your life, you've made someone laugh. Maybe it was unintentional, maybe it was something small. But you know that feeling. You wouldn't be here if you didn't. It's an oddly magical feeling. It's pure, primal validation and it feels so good. I remember the first time I felt it. I was 13 years old, and I don't remember what I said, all I remember was that feeling of acceptance. I knew I wanted more of that. The only problem was, I had no idea what I had said. I didn't know why or how I made them laugh, but I knew I had to figure it out.

This launched me on a lifelong mission: I became determined to understand funny. I wanted to know not just how to make people laugh, but *why* it makes them laugh. Why doesn't everyone laugh at the same things? Why do my parents laugh at things I don't even understand? I wanted to unravel it all. I I could understand *why* things were funny, I could start to create funny things on my own. And then if I could understand everything about funny, I could figure theoretically make anyone laugh. Of course, that isn't how it viewed it at the time. All I really knew is that if I could make people laugh, I could make people like me.

I started paying attention when people laughed at anything. No matter how small or insignificant, I wanted to figure out what caused that reaction. I was a little creep; I'd eavesdrop on conversations and spy on people from a distance. I'd put on headphones with no music so people didn't think I could hear them. Little by little I started to pick up things. It was difficult at first because humor is so subjective. Unexpected things would make people laugh, but so would very familiar things. I'd see the same thing said two different ways and one would make people laugh and the other would make them angry. Slowly I started to learn small tricks that could elicit laughter, and I started to emulate them. I failed a lot, lived through a lot of uncomfortable moments, and made more than a few people angry, but I made progress. Slowly and methodically, I got funnier. By the time I was a senior in high school, I was legitimately kind of funny. Without being very popular, I was voted class president on the back of an unexpectedly funny speech. It was my first glimpse at how making people laugh can go even further than making them like you. It can make them trust you and believe in you. This was the

If you look at my life now, it's obvious that being funny has been a huge advantage. I've toured the world as a stand-up comedian, made dozens of TV appearances, and paid my rent for years off of being funny. But what isn't obvious is what being funny has done for me in my day-to-day life. I was an awkward, nerdy kid destined for a quiet life of few friends and less fun. But learning how to be funny started opening social doors, and now I have the confidence to enter any situation knowing that I'll leave with new friends.

One of the greatest benefits gained from become funny is confidence. I've never been a trained fighter, but I imagine it's a similar feeling. Fighters know they can go anywhere and handle any physical situation that may arise. Being funny is the same, but socially instead of physically. I know that whatever situation comes up, I can talk my way out of it. I can defuse the tension and relax the atmosphere and we can all go home unharmed. Once you understand how to make people laugh, you become confident that whatever situation arises, you can charm your way through it. Maybe it's not as cool as being able to kick the crap out of people, but it's a lot less work.

With that confidence, and the goods to back it up, you'll notice a change in your life. The funnier I got; the easier life got. Things are a lot less stressful. For instance, I look forward to job interviews. They're a chance to show off my skills. They're a chance for me to make this person like me so much that they'll offer me the job, even if I'm not the most qualified. If an employer really likes you, they'll find a place for you. I've been a stand-up comedian for a long time, and entertainment income ebbs and flows – sometimes there are lean years that necessitate another job. Despite my resume saying I'm a clown, my side gigs have always been good gigs. I've worked for investment software companies, hotel booking companies, voice security companies – I've had several jobs that could easily be lifelong careers. And every one of them I've been under qualified for. But I can honestly say that since I put my mind to being funny, I've never once gone to an interview and not been offered a job. There are lots of times I haven't gotten an interview, but if I can get in front of them, I'll get the job. Sure, sometimes it's a horrible mistake and they regret it, but I always get the offer. That is the power of funny.

Relationships are no different - both romantic and friendly. People gravitate towards friendly people. Life is, generally, kind of shitty. So, if you're the type of person that always sparks joy, people want to be around you. And if you can learn the art of empathetic humor – making the laughs about your audience instead of yourself – your connections will grow even more meaningful. You can make people feel like you really understand them, and that kind of feeling is impossible to ignore. By learning how to take the information that you're given and turn it into uplifting humor you become the kind of person people can't get enough of. If you can make everyone you meet feel special you'll never be lonely again.

This book is designed to help give you these tools. This is meant to be a shortcut to understanding why things are funny, and how to exploit that to create humor out of whatever information you're given. It will show you the techniques that you'll need to practice to be consistently funny, regardless of your audience. But what this book can't do is make you instantly funny on it's own. That's like reading a workout book and expecting to be ripped by the end of it. It's not how it goes - you must put in the work. Being funny is the same way. You must change the way you think and the way you observe, and that doesn't happen overnight. But I guarantee that if you take these tools and practice them, **you will be funny.**

The most important thing I've learned on my journey to understanding funny is that making someone laugh is more about them than it is about you. To make a single person laugh, you have to understand how that person thinks. Each person has a very different sense of humor, based on their experiences and feelings. If you want to make that person laugh, you have to pay attention to them. You have to be a good listener if you truly want to connect. The keys to being funny are easy: listen, empathize, edit. You want to take in information about the person, empathize with their position and their beliefs, and then edit your own instincts to match theirs.

It's a bit counter intuitive, because the funny we are used to seeing is the opposite. We're used to seeing a comedian onstage or in a video talking about themselves. It's all about the performer, and not about the listener. But that is a different environment. Making an audience laugh is way different than making a human being laugh. To make a single person laugh you need to be as specific as possible. The more connected they are to the material, the more it will affect them. Once you can learn to exploit this you can learn to make a deep meaningful connection with practically anyone.

Sound too good to be true? Well, like everything, there is a catch. Everyone can become that kind of funny, but it takes work. It's not easy to re-wire your brain to think in funny. It means looking at every situation differently than you do currently. You need to take a *humor first* approach in which you look for funny first before anything else.

As though that isn't enough, you also have to take chances. In order to get better you have to try things and see what works. At some point you're going to annoy someone. At some point you're going to offend someone. At some point you're going to flop a joke and deal with abject silence. You have to simply take it on the chin, learn from it, and move on. It's not easy: if it was, everyone would be funny. I'm going to show you some simple tricks that will help build your confidence, but for this to really work, I mean life changing work, you have to put in the effort. There's no shortcut.

The goal of the book you are about to read is as follows: I want to make you understand *why* things are funny. What makes people laugh? Then I want to show you how to take that knowledge and apply it. Once you know why people laugh, how can you manipulate that to your benefit? When we have those skills in place, I will teach you how to apply them for different situations.

- I'll show you how to be funny in a professional setting to make your bosses and coworkers love you. It's often hard to maintain a professional air and still crack jokes, but doing so can make you indispensable in the office.
- I'll teach you some tricks to making friends with humour. How to be self deprecating in the proper way, and how to playfully rib people and encourage them to rib you.
- I'll impart on you how to flirt with humour. From how to craft a unique icebreaker to how to be complimentary funny. It's not easy to give a straight compliment sometimes, but you can hide it in a joke to stifle the awkwardness.

Throughout the book you'll stumble upon an assortment of exercises to provide some hands-on training along your journey. The exercises are broken into three different categories:

> **Train Your Brain:** Direct exercises where you'll need to craft jokes or thoughts from your own brain.
>
> **Get a Laugh Right Now:** Ways to use what you just learned immediately to make real world people laugh.
>
> **Mull it over:** Thought exercises for you to reflect on to guide you how to think funny.

These direct, practical exercises will help you take the theory and make it a reality. Instead of just telling you how it works, these bonus sections will let you work the muscles needed to get laughs.

Additionally, the book is broken into two sections: the first half of the book is theoretical. We'll go over the theory behind what makes people laugh, why it makes them laugh, and the mechanics behind the jokes. We'll then go through the conceptual idea of *creating funny.* You'll learn techniques and theories that can be used to make funny moments and present yourself as a funny, smart person. We'll go over the basics of wit and look at how you need to think to present yourself as clever. The essence of the first half is that we are creating a set of tools and ideas that are the building blocks of being funny.

The second half of the book is more practical. I'll take you through real life situations and teach you how you can best use humor to better yourself. I'll show you tangible examples of how to be funny and give you ideas you can use right way. I'll go through work, friends, and romance and look at the differences in approach you should be taking to get laughs in each situation. This will show you how by examining your environment you can optimize your humor to get the maximum result.

Throughout the book you'll also run into a variety of interactive sections that will help you actively train your brain to look for and find the funny in as many situations as possible. I'll give you practical exercises that will sharpen your skills, as well as thought patterns that will turn your thoughts into jokes. I'll also give you jokes and joke formats that you can use immediately to get laughs right now.

The main goal is to change your way of thinking so that you're always ready to be funny. If you're not actively thinking about humour in your day-to-day life, you're selling yourself short. You and everyone around you could be having a lot more fun, and you won't believe the rewards.

Here we go.

Part 1: Theoretically Funny

I've been a stand-up comedian for over 15 years and in that decade and a half I've met thousands and thousands of people who were all trying to be funny. In that time, I've learned this above all else: Most people don't understand why something is funny. They know **when** something is funny, but not **why** it's funny. It makes creating funny a whole lot more difficult since you have to essentially wait for a funny thought or experience. But if you understand why things are funny then you can actively create funny things instead of waiting for their arrival. It's the difference between being one of those fish who sits on the ocean floor waiting for prey to swim by and being a shark that goes out hunting for whatever it wants.

There are lots of ways to make people laugh, but they all center around **context, surprise, and expectation**. By understanding how to recognize and manipulate these three things you can create funny out of nothing. There are many tips and tricks to get laughs, but they center around these three concepts.

This section will show you how to analyze and understand funny moments. We will peel back the curtain and show the techniques that are used to make you laugh. Humor may be subjective, but the physical mechanisms used to make people laugh are not. Almost all jokes use the same formats but with different subject matter. It's like how movies, regardless of genre, have a very similar structure. Being able to recognize and then apply these techniques is what it takes to become funny yourself.

By starting from the bottom and learning humor from the ground up you can be prepared for any situation. You can be confident that no matter what comes up, you have the tools to make it funny.

Let's get a look at those tools

Chapter 1 - What is funny?

The first step in being a funny person is to understand funny, and that's more complicated than it sounds. Think about it: you always know **that** something is funny, but if you try to figure out **why**, it gets tricky. Why is a guy getting hit in the nuts with a ball funny, but getting hit with a hammer upsetting? What object is the nut-shot breaking point where it becomes no longer funny? A watermelon? A bat? It's murky at best.

It becomes even less clear when we factor in the subjective nature of comedy. Why do I laugh at some things when others don't? Since everyone finds different things funny, you might think it's impossible to nail down why we laugh. But that simply isn't the case. In fact, while we all laugh at different **content**, the **mechanisms** that make us laugh are more universal.

Laughter is a physical reaction that can be brought on by a few different stimuli, but the main factors are surprise and relief of tension. If your strait-laced cop friend comes out of nowhere and says, *"Hey you wanna go smoke some crack in my attic?"* you might laugh, because you wouldn't expect him to say that. Our brain finds that surprise amusing and causes us to laugh. Similarly, if you walk into your house and a shadowy figure yells *Police, get on the fucking ground and lick the floor*, you might be terrified. Your **expectation** is that you're about to be murdered. But you might laugh when your friend turns on the light and reveals it was him playing a prank on you. The relief brought on by the release of that tension when our expectations are shown to be wrong causes us to laugh.

As you start to investigate what makes things funny, you'll find that most often the actual laughter is induced by surprise or relief tension. These aren't the only ways to get people to laugh - we'll go over some others later - but they are the main core mechanisms for laughter. Let's go through an example to better illustrate what I mean by these concepts. According to Reader's Digest, this joke was voted funniest across several different languages. I like it because it's an easy-to-understand example.

We're going to tear it apart to see why it's funny:

Maybe you find that funny, maybe you don't. To be quite honest, it doesn't matter. It's something a lot of people find funny, so to understand what makes people laugh, you have to understand why it's funny. You have to recognize why people are laughing **regardless of your own personal tastes**. Humor is subjective, and you need to see beyond your own self if you want to make others laugh.

So, what is funny about the joke? We start by breaking down the part that makes people laugh - the punchline. In this case, the punchline is:

There's a silence, then a shot. Back on the phone, the guy says, "OK, now what?"

If you take that away, there's nothing funny about the joke - it's just a sad story told with very strange wording. The punchline is where the surprise is revealed, and the tension is broken. The surprise must be hidden until the last moment to induce the reaction. In this case, we induce surprise by misdirecting the listener. The listener thinks that the operator is telling the hunter to check to see if his friend is breathing. The surprise is that the hunter thinks the operator is telling him that if he isn't dead already, kill him. The humor comes from the surprise of the gunshot, and the release of tension with the hunter's words. But why is that funny? Let's break it down by looking at what I believe are the key ingredients to making someone laugh.

1.1 Context

There is nothing more important to something being funny than the context. The person who is supposed to laugh must have all of the background knowledge needed to understand the joke, otherwise it's meaningless. Sometimes something happens that we find absolutely hilarious, but when we try to tell it to people, they don't laugh. It's the classic "*I guess you had to be there*" situation. That person doesn't laugh because they don't have the context to see why the thing was funny.

Look at the hunting joke again. Think about what you have to know to get it, and keep in mind that this was specifically written so as many people get it as possible. You have to know what hunters are, that they would have guns, and what 'the woods' are. Most people know that, but if you were a child in a desert area where hunting is mainly done with spears, you're going to have a hard time getting this. You have to know that 911 is the number to dial for emergency assistance, which is not how it works in most of the world (in the UK, for instance, the number is 999). And if you've never heard the phrase "make sure he's dead" in reference to killing someone, you would be confused. So, you can see immediately that there are people who won't find this joke funny regardless of their sense of humor. They simply lack the context to be able to *get* it.

This is the absolute most basic level of context. The audience needs to literally understand the words, phrases, and ideas that you're saying to understand the joke. It sounds trivial, but it's incredibly important. When you're crafting a joke, you need to speak about things your audience understands.

Context goes much deeper than this, however. For instance: a person's beliefs need to match up with the beliefs of a joke. If you make a joke where the inference is that Donald Trump is a moron to a Donald Trump fan, they're not going to laugh. Context is far more than just understanding the phrases and references, it goes to a person's core.

We'll have a much more in-depth conversation about context later. For now, it's enough to focus on understanding what the words and phrases mean.

1.2 Expectation/Surprise

Laughter is a visceral reaction, like being scared. So regardless of whether you're telling a joke or a story, the funny part should be a surprise. And the best way to surprise someone is to misdirect their expectations. Sort of like how a magician will wave a wand to distract you from what he's doing in his other hand. You want to lead the listener/reader to be thinking one thing, and then surprise them with a turnaround. So, in this joke, the entire set up is designed to make people think that the hunter is doing everything he can to save his friend. This warps our thinking so that when we hear "Let's make sure he's dead" we are automatically trained to assume that he will check his friend's heartbeat or breathing. This makes it a huge surprise when the hunter shoots his friend. By managing our expectations, the joke creates surprise.

This is why jokes don't work when you hear them over and over again. There is no surprise, so you don't have that reaction. It's like if you went for a drive one day and saw this:

You'd probably laugh. But if drove by it every single day for years you simply wouldn't. Surprise is a big part of comedy.

The more you venture into the world of funny, the more you'll come to appreciate the element of surprise. And ironically, the more that you prepare, the easier it is to surprise someone. It takes practice. Before you share a funny anecdote, or even just a funny snippit, think about it first. Say it in your head a few times, and rearrange it so the funny part is as surprising as possible. If you're telling a story, you have to actively think of drawing the listener one way and then surprise them with the punch in a different direction. Surprise is the mechanism that takes something humorous, and elicits laughter. Let's look at the same joke, but with the surprise removed:

Two hunters are out in the woods when one of them collapses. He's not breathing and his eyes are glazed. The other guy whips out his cell phone and calls 911.

"I think my friend is dead!" he yells. "What can I do?"

The operator says, "Calm down. First, let's make sure he's dead."

The hunter misunderstood the operator and due to the poor choice of wording, believed that the operator meant that if his friend was still alive that he would have to complete the kill. He didn't want to do that, but the operator was the professional, so he begrudgingly listened. He steadied himself, pulled the trigger, and then sadly returned to the phone to continue on the process.

By over explaining each step we remove the surprise element, and the whole thing becomes a lot less funny. When you're creating a funny moment, you need to ensure that the twist is a surprise.

The more you learn to figure out the root of funny, the more you'll realize it's almost always due to surprise. Even comedy that you don't realize is using surprise and expectation is, like physical comedy or absurdism. Both only work because we have an expectation of how things are supposed to be. Our expectation is that a person can walk easily across a room, so when he trips and falls on his face, it's a surprise and we laugh. Comedy is all about expectation and surprise, right down to the dumbest jokes you've heard.

Why did the chicken cross the road?

To get to the other side!

This joke only works because of our expectations. Think about it.

Why did the chicken cross the road?

Most English speaking, western raised human beings this is the setup for a joke. We've heard this format many times. An obscure question asked with a sly smile implying that it isn't meant to be answered earnestly. So, we are **expecting** a joke. We know it's a setup, we're waiting for the funny twist. But the twist is that there is no twist. It's called an anti-joke, because it preys on your understanding of joke structure. It takes that expectation and subverts it by not giving you a joke. If you're not a native English speaker and are not familiar with that tired joke structure, then *to get to the other side* seems like an obvious statement of fact. You tell that joke to a native German and you're going to get nothing. Although to be fair, you tell any joke to a native German and you'll probably get nothing.

I don't think there's a better example of expectation and surprise in comedy than the **rule of three**. The rule of three basically means that it takes three different examples to properly execute a surprise in a list of similar things. How it works is that the first two examples set a pattern that sets the pattern in the listener's brain, and then the third example breaks the pattern and surprises the listener. It sounds basic, but it's used everywhere. For example:

My three favourite days of the year are my Thanksgiving, Christmas, and McDonald's McRib Day

The first two set up the expectation that I am naming holidays, then the third breaks that and the surprise is pleasant to us. Learning how to manage expectation and surprise is learning the art of funny.

Get a Laugh RIGHT NOW
Exploiting the rule of 3 for instant jokes

Rule of 3 can be a great way to get a laugh off a mundane question. Here are some examples.

"Hey! How was your weekend?"
"Oh you know, pretty typical. We took the kids to see their grandparents, went out to dinner, sacrificed a hobo to the god Cthulu, standard weekend stuff."

"What are your plans for the holiday?"
"Gonna take it slow. Clean out the garage, get some yardwork done, maybe make some babies with Emma Stone if I have the time."

"Have you been watching anything good on TV?"
"Oh yeah, I've been watching some classics lately. Sopranos, The Wire, that kid on youtube that buttchuggs energy drinks."

Advanced technique:
If you've mastered the rule of three and are looking to kick things up a notch, here is the next step in the rule of three: use your third example as not just a punchline, but also the setup to a follow-up joke. You do this by making the third example different enough to shock out a laugh, but vague enough that it requires a follow up question. Then your explanation for the third example is also a joke. It sounds a bit complicated, but it looks like this:

"You like movies? What are your favourites?"
"I like the real artsy underdog ones. You know, Rain Man, Rudy, that one where they force that mentally challenged guy to fight everybody."
"What one was that?"
"Oh what's it called... Rocky"

By using a third example that is designed to elicit a response you can then prepare a follow up joke. This makes it seem like you're much faster and funnier on your feet than you really are. Try it out!

1.3 Suspense/Relief

Surprise can be even more heightened when it's paired with tension. If the surprise also washes the audience's worry away, you get a double shot of feelings. So, to elicit more of a response from someone, you want to build the tension. The bigger the build up of suspense, the more primal the release will be. Think about when you scare someone – once they realize it's a prank and not real danger, the most common response is to laugh. Nothing funny has happened per se, but the release of that tension causes our bodies to laugh. The worry we had melts away and that relief is such a nice feeling that we can't help but laugh. When you combine that with an actual humorous surprise the results are astounding. We can use this principle in jokes to add extra spice to our punchlines. Let's go back to our example joke, specifically this line:

There's a silence, then a shot. Back on the phone, the guy says, "OK, now what?"

The way this is phrased is to add more suspense to the punchline. Instead of having the hunter simply walk over and shoot the other, the author adds: 'There's a silence, then a shot'. The silence adds suspense as the listener/reader figures out what the silence is, and then what the shot is. This build up adds to the release when the reader figures out what actually happened.

Tension can be built in a lot of ways: it's the basis for cringe humour for example. The Office is funny because of its discomfort and the tension that builds. Dark humour is similar; it's often not the material that is funny but the audacity to say something awful. These tools can be useful, but if you often find that the crux of the humor is from tension it can become uncomfortable for most people. Especially in North America. The American version of the office deviates from the constant cringe of the original, and that made it far more palatable for a wider audience.

The relief of tension heightens our emotions in a number of ways, which is why you see strange reactions from people after tense situations. Like after an accident, or after a confrontation. People will sometimes laugh because that release is so powerful. It's why fail videos are so popular, but only so when it's clear the people are not seriously hurt. It's that build up of tension as we wait to see what happens, then a release when it's over. By harnessing this and adding tension and suspense to our jokes and stories we can create a much more powerful response.

1.4 External Factors

As I mentioned earlier, context is more than simply knowing what the joke is about. Another huge factor is the current environment that you're in. It's impossible to understate how much whatever is going on around you affects your sense of humor. Sometimes certain things are funny only in very specific situations, and it's important to recognize this. For instance, if you're over tired you may find things hilarious that you wouldn't normally laugh at. Or, say, you and a small number of people share a space for an extended time. Perhaps a weekend in a small cabin. That shared context creates an environment where things might only be funny for that moment. It's important to assess the environment and determine how much of the laughter is due to the setting.

I'm not saying it's not funny, just maybe not at Mom's Funeral

As a stand-up comedian, we have to do comedy in a lot of different venues. Bars, restaurants, legions, community centers, people's yards, my own nightmares. But the best is always comedy clubs. Because in that atmosphere people know they are supposed to laugh, and they are prepared for it. This allows things to get laughs that simply wouldn't if you were at a party.

External factors simply can't be ignored when explaining why something is funny.

Maybe the most important of all external factors that you should investigate is this: **are other people laughing.** According to nerds who do science:

"If you see two people laughing at a joke you didn't hear, chances are you will smile anyway--even if you don't realize it."
– livescience.com

Its why sitcoms have a laugh track. It sounds dumb, but it's important to keep in mind. Basically, if you're in a group of friends and you're all laughing, chances are good that whatever you're laughing at isn't as funny as you think. The group laughter dynamic heightens the experience and skews your perspective. This is a double-edged sword – while things you come up with in a group may not be funny enough to transport to another conversation, but abusing the idea of group laughter you can build memorable moments from less than optimal conditions.

The point is: when evaluating the funniness of something, you need to account for external factors.

Mull it Over

Control what you can, use what you can't

External factors are, in general, out of your control. But here are some things you can do:

Laugh: as I mentioned above, if you hear people laughing, chances are good you will be too. So to facilitate other people laughing, be a good laugher yourself.

Acknowledge: If something would be funny except that you're at a funeral, acknowledge that. *If we weren't at a funeral, I would be straight roasting those awful shoes of yours.* The joke is now that you can't make the joke because of external factors. This gives you the surprise of the joke built on the tension of the external factors.

Save it for later: Similar to acknowledging, but past tense: *I wanted to make fun of that lady's hat so bad, but the priest was right beside me.* The rehashed tension is great fodder for laughter.

Touch Base: if you can't make jokes with anyone in the situation, use the situation to make jokes to people outside. Text others to talk about the external factors. The tension from an ongoing situation can be used to make humor.

Always be aware of what is going on around you and use it to your advantage.

1.5 Cleverness

Like repetition, there's something in our brains that responds to something we find exceedingly clever with laughter. Cleverness can come in many forms, from large scope observations all the way down to the lowly pun. Cleverness is like charisma, it's hard to define but you know it when you see it.

For something to be clever, there has to be a logical leap made. Essentially, you have to show the audience something that they couldn't see for themselves, but once they've seen it, it's obvious. The fact that you can see something they couldn't is what is perceived as clever.

Think of this riddle:

What is seen in the middle of March and April that can't be seen at the beginning or end of either month?

The answer is the letter r.

It's obvious once you see it, but it's hard to make the leap on your own. Jokes are very similar to riddles, except that they lean more towards funny than clever. So, the logical leap isn't always to an answer that is satisfying, but one that is surprising. For instance, contrast this dumb joke with the previous riddle:

Why do we tell actors to break a leg?

Answer: Because every play has to have a cast

It's not nearly as satisfying because the answer doesn't make a ton of logical sense. However, it does make enough sense for the listener to make the connection. That bit of logic mixed with absurdity is the structural concept behind most jokes. The more logical the leap, the cleverer. Too clever and you've got yourself a riddle. Too absurd and you've got yourself nonsense. Balance is everything when it comes to clever.

1.6 Other Techniques

While surprise, expectation and context are the main drivers of laughter, there are a number of techniques that assist in making things funnier. Think of surprise and tension as the engine of the car and these techniques as everything else. You don't need a seat to make a car move, but it makes it a hell of a lot more comfortable. These techniques are ways to make your jokes more streamlined and effective. I'll cover a couple that are essential to the example joke and then a bunch that aren't. The more you can identify these techniques the more you will start to get an appreciation for the art of making something funny.

Timing

As a stand-up comedian, you end up having to host a lot of shows and events, and one of the things you learn very early is that when you say something is often more important to laughter than what you say. One of the best ways to seem clever is to have responses ready immediately. It doesn't have to be perfect if the quickness is impressive on its own.

This works for us in a couple of different ways. The first is that you can people are impressed when you can put together thoughts quickly. If someone says something to you, and you can respond with a half coherent retort before you should have had time to process the sentence, people will be impressed. And if you can learn to do that with the proper tone and at the right times, you can easily turn that into laughter.

Here are a couple of dumb examples that I use in everyday life, just to give you an idea of what I mean. These are both really stupid, and not very funny objectively, but by using these timing tricks I can appear clever.

When someone tells me something that is clearly extraordinary or weird about themselves, whether it's something they do or somewhere they're from, I pretend I already knew that. For instance:

Me: "What do you do for a living?"
Them: "I'm actually a doctor in marine biology specializing in revitalizing collapsing coral reefs"
Me: "Oh weird that's exactly what I was going to guess"

When someone tells you their job, and it's an uncommon one, they expect a reaction from you. They expect you to be surprised and a bit impressed. If you immediately act the opposite, then for a second, they wonder how you could possibly know that about them. That's the surprise factor we're talking about above. And it also plays into the release of tension, because when they realize you're joking, there is a relief that you aren't inside their head. This triggers a laugh in most people. Some people might hate you, but that's the risk of trying to be funny.

It's not brilliantly funny, but it's enough that with perfect timing, you can catch someone off guard and get a laugh. I'll show you more practical examples, and how to construct your own later.

Mull it Over
Timing is everything

One of the easiest ways to get laughs is to have quick reactions to shared events. The classic example is being in a restaurant when a waiter drops a plate. Everyone hears it and everyone briefly stops. Inevitably, someone yells "**Just put that anywhere**" and everyone laughs.

But how do you come up with a lightning quick, perfectly timed response? The secret: think of it ahead of time.

When an event happens like a plate drop that stops everything for that brief second, reflect on it. Think of what would've been funny if you had said it right away. You're going to miss the moment this time, but next time you'll have that on hand right away.

Don't be afraid to use a pre-prepared line in a situation that isn't exactly perfect either. The main catalyst for laughter here is the tension caused by the shared event. In that brief, quiet instance, no one is quite sure what to do. Breaking that tension with an immediate joke, even a non-ideal one, results in laughter of relief.

The timing has to be perfect, the joke does not.

Think about it!

Brevity

Brevity is the soul of wit

It's an adage from the Mark Twain days, but it still holds true today. The more you muddy up your joke with extra words the less impact it has on the audience. Extraneous details are the death of comedy. If you want to make people laugh, you want to cut out all the fat and get right to the funny part. First, it keeps people interested. If you add too many details, people get bored. They get distracted, they lose focus, and you're not going to get them laughing at the end because they're no longer invested in the joke. We showed earlier how a much wordier punchline doesn't work nearly as well, but extra words in the setup are a problem too. Let's look at the joke again, but this time let's keep the same punchline, so the funny part is the same. But let's see what happens when we add unnecessary details to the set up.

Two hunters, Steve and David, are walking through the back country of North Dakota. It's a remote wooded area known for its wildlife, an excellent place for hunting. All of the sudden David, with his pre-existing heart condition, starts to convulse, and after a minute collapse to the ground. Steve rushes over to investigate, only to find that David isn't breathing, and his eyes have glazed over. Steve isn't a doctor, but he knows that's quite bad. He wipes away tears as he fumbles for his cell phone, an old Samsung that doesn't get service at the best of times. Panicky, he walks in circles looking for a signal. When he finally, he sees that bar appear, he frantically dials 9-11.

A middle-aged woman with a soothing voice answers and asks Steve what the emergency is. Steve is so scared he's yelling into the phone: "I think my friend is dead!" he takes a labored breath. "What can I do?" The well-trained operator knows that Steve isn't much help in his worked up state, so she tries to settle him down. "Calm down." she says. "First, let's make sure he's dead."

There's a silence, then a shot. Back on the phone, the guy says,

"OK, now what?"

It's the same joke, but if someone tried to tell you all that you'd need a nap before the punchline. Even if they want to enjoy the joke the extra details make it confusing to know what to focus on. The unnecessary information is an overload and listening to the story becomes work to follow.

It's a mistake I see a lot of people make when they try to be funny. They try to stay as true to the story as possible by adding every little detail. It feels right because you want to paint a full picture, but you need to boil it down to the essence. Especially when you're just learning to be funny, you want to take a story or a joke or an anecdote and reduce it down to just the funny parts. Any extraneous details should be left out, unless they are jokes in their own right.

If I'm telling a joke, I don't include anything unless:

    a) it's vital to the understanding of the story
    b) it's funny on its own.

The more you can stick to this principle, the better your jokes will land.

Distance

Another old corny phrase you might be familiar with is this:

Comedy = Tragedy + Time

Basically, as you get further from a horrible event, the funnier it seems. Take this for instance: in 1919 there was a horrible tragedy in Boston. A storage tank holding a buttload of fermented molasses exploded, sending a tidal wave of sticky goo through the surrounding area. It destroyed buildings and killed 21 people. In 1919 Boston, there was nothing funny about that. The great molasses flood was a tragedy that crippled. But now, 100 years later in any other town, the Great Molasses Flood is hilarious. I mean come on, *slow as old molasses* is a saying for a reason, how did 21 of them get caught by it?

In this equation, it's important to note that "Time" doesn't always mean *time* in the way that we know it. Think of it more as mental distance from what happened. If you hear that a guy halfway across the world that you've never met and will never meet got his penis bitten off by a wombat – that's kind of funny. If it was your husband - not so much. That mental distance allows for laughter.

Again, let's go back to our hunting joke. Technically speaking, if you take the joke at face value it's not really a joke at all, it's a retelling of a tragic story told in a funny way. The actual content is horrible. This poor hunter watches his friend die, and then thinks he needs to put a bullet in him. It's haunting. But the way it's told distances us from the actual content. In a way, it's manufacturing that distance so that this tragedy is funny. Let's look at how they do it.

Two hunters are out in the woods…

Immediately the author has set to work establishing mental distance. This is a very cold way to describe the lead characters in our story. By calling them two hunters out in the woods, they've already established these guys are faceless characters. By not giving them names or defining features, or even a real backdrop the humanity has been sucked out of them, which gives the space needed for us to find their awful situation funny. If this is a story you're telling about a real hunter with a real family and real kids, there is nothing funny about it. If the joke ended with the second hunter's crying family huddled over his dead body screaming *"why God? Why?"* you probably wouldn't laugh. But by adding layers of abstraction, we give the listener the freedom to assume that this is not real, that this is a joke. Also, the wording in the dialogue is stiff and a bit forced, which is another way to muddy the water and let the listener know they are hearing a joke.

Now, I understand that you're not going to be relaying tragedies as funny all that often, but this technique holds true for another very important aspect of social comedy: self deprecation. Taking shots at yourself is one of the easiest ways to disarm people and make yourself seem likeable. We'll discuss this more in depth later on, but the concept of distance that we've brought up is vital. I use self deprecation a lot in conversation, and it's an incredibly useful tool. But one mistake I see people make far too often is that they are too close to what they are trying to make fun of. They actually hurt themselves with their jokes, and people can tell. If you're going to make fun of something about yourself, you'd better be confident about it. Even if behind the scenes it bothers you, you can't show that. The jokes have to be confidently negative, if that makes any sense.

For instance, I'm a bit overweight, and I like to poke fun at that. But it took me a while to be able to do it in such a way that it didn't seem like I was being a big fat sad guy. The difference is displaying confidence. Like if someone asks me if I want to take the stairs, I'll often say with mock anger:

Hey, you don't get a body like this by taking the stairs.

It catches people off guard, and usually gets a laugh. Compare that to jokes I used to try when I was more self conscious about my weight. Back then I'd try things like:

Fat me will probably die on those stairs.

There's a world of difference in how those two lines are taken. The second one is tinged with sadness and gives off the air that I'm actively upset about my weight. The first, on the other hand, steals a phrase that is used to celebrate fitness and co-opts it. That extra added twist, and the surprise from it, let people know that I'm joking. And the way I distance myself from the jab makes it feel less sad.

If the funny comes from tragedy, try to put as much distance between your audience and the victim as possible.

Hyperbole

The definition of hyperbole is *exaggeration not intended to deceive*. The concept is to surprise the audience with your over-the-top description. But in order for it to work it has to be so over the top that they couldn't possibly believe it was real. The humor comes from the unexpected way that you describe the thing in question. *I'm hungry enough to eat a horse*, is the classic example. The audience doesn't believe that you could eat a horse, but they are so surprised by your description of how hungry you are that it's funny. You can use this for anything, and it's an easy way to insert laughs into regular conversation. For example:

It's so hot outside that hell would be a welcome relief.

Or

I'm so thirsty I would drink the sweat from a fat guy's bellybutton

You're saying something you would say seriously, but the hyperbole gives it an extra little kick. It's never going to be a *bring the house down* kind of laugh, but it can consistently make whatever you're saying substantially funnier.

Get a Laugh RIGHT NOW
Exaggerate your way to laughter

Whenever you're describing an amount of something, keep hyperbole in mind.

Instead of saying: "I slept great last night"
Try saying: "I slept so much last night I think it technically counts as a coma"

Instead of saying: "That meeting was so long"
Try saying: "That meeting was so long that all of the cells in my body have died and regenerated so I'm actually a whole new person now."

Instead of saying: "The restaurant was busy"
Try saying: "I'm pretty sure the entire population of Sudbury was at IHOP last night."

Advanced tip: Hyperbole isn't always crazy hilarious on its own. Use it as a setup to a follow up joke.

"I'm pretty sure the entire population of Sudbury was at IHOP last night. At least it smelled like it."

By using your hyperbole to set up a second joke, you double up on your laughter.

Sarcasm/Irony

For our purposes I'm going to define sarcasm as saying something with the implication that it is inherently false, for the purposes of humor.

> *"I got a D- on my Math exam, hand me*
> *that MENSA application."*

The humor comes from our brain making the connection that the statement is an intended falsehood. So our initial reaction in our brain is to say "Oh man this guy is so stupid he thinks he's smart!" Then once your brain processes the irony, it understands that it's been had, and that causes a spark in us. We like the trick, and we laugh.

Sarcasm is a good tool, but it relies entirely on the audience's awareness of the irony. It can be difficult to tell if something is sarcastic because it depends so much on the audience's perspective. When analyzing something for sarcasm, try to put yourself in the shoes of the author.

For instance:

> *"What a beautiful day, let's thank the good Lord for all*
> *he provides us and bask in the delights he's offered us"*

It's probably sarcastic if it's said by an atheist, but probably sincere coming from a nun. Sarcasm requires a firm sense of who is speaking and what they believe. As such, it can be one of the more complicated forms of humor to understand.

Silliness/Absurdity: People have been laughing at clowns and Mr. Bean for as long as I can remember, because people like silliness. It's a slightly different form of surprise but it's the same principle. The clown ends up pie-ing himself in the face and we laugh at the absurdity because no one does that kind of thing. There's also a bit of tragedy as the clown gets pied, but the big painted smile on his face tells you it's ok.

The laughter is always from an action that we don't expect to happen, or from manufactured tension broken in an absurd way. Basically if you find yourself thinking *what the fuck was that* while you're laughing, you're looking at silliness.

Repetition/Familiarity

I know I've done nothing but harp on about how important surprise is, and rightfully so, but it's not the only avenue for laughter. Sort of on the opposite end of the spectrum is the use of repetition. This method isn't showcased in the joke, but it's important to talk about because it's incredibly useful in conversation. Our brains are wired to be very sensitive to repetition. All music is repetition, and we're naturally tuned to that. It's important to pattern recognition and pattern recognition is pretty vital to everything that we do. Because of this, our brain reacts very odd to certain kinds of repetition, and we can exploit that to make things funny. At a base level we've all experienced this, we've all said a word so many times that it lost all meaning and became hilarious. Say the word mayonnaise 100 times in a row and try not to laugh. Life loses all meaning around 75.

Famous comedians like George Carlin and Chris Rock repeat things over and over again. It cements into people's brains and becomes funny. And repetition works well with suspense, because after a certain number of repetitions, you build expectation. People are now anticipating that repetition, so you can hold it back and build suspense. Think about all the movies and TV shows that show you the ending first, then flash back to the start. You know how it's going to end, but the suspense is in how you get there. You can do that with humor as well. I'll explain more thoroughly with practical examples later on in the book.

Along the same lines, familiarity is a wonderful tool not just to get laughs, but also to up your likeability. And what I mean by familiarity is this – using something that the listener has personally thought to connect with them. So, for example, reference based humor. One of the easiest ways to get a laugh from someone is to repeat something they already found funny. People will sit around for hours and quote their favourite lines from funny shows or movies. By working these into your interactions, it makes the listener aware that you have had a shared experience, and subconsciously draws them closer to you. Many (especially male) friendships are built on nothing more than laughing at the same things over and over again.

But there's a deeper level to familiarity than just quoting The Simpsons to your friends. To me, the two greatest jokes in the world are built like this:

- A thought that no one has ever had before
- A thought that everyone has had but no one has spoken.

If you are able to crystallize someone's thoughts and speak it back to them in a funny way, it creates a connection like you wouldn't believe. It's the equivalent of showing someone that they aren't alone, but without the cheesy awkwardness. Obviously you can't have this kind of intimate understanding of a person's thoughts without knowing them, but we can expand on that concept and apply it to a group of people instead of an individual.

All that rambling basically boils down to this: people like hearing about themselves. The more personal, the better. It makes us feel less alone. So one of the best ways to make people laugh is to make it about them. If you're talking to a firefighter, include that in your thought process. And I don't mean make jokes about fires. If you're going to joke to a firefighter about fires, you better know a goddamn lot about fires. This better be a serious, inside fire knowledge that only you and a firefighter would know. What I mean is that you should take into consideration the perspective a firefighter might have on things as you speak. We'll discuss how to apply this practically later in the book.

One of the best ways, comedically speaking, to utilize familiarity to get laughs is through analogies. Analogies are some of the most powerful literary tools available, used by everyone from Shakespeare to Kid Rock. Our brains are great at understanding things in terms of things we already understand, if that makes sense. It instantly clicks in our brains and releases some of that good stuff. If it's both unexpected and appropriate enough, you'll get a laugh. Look at almost any roast joke. They are analogies relating someone's looks/weight/age/etc to something else we can picture, and the results speak for themselves.

Mull it over
Seeing the world through analogies

Analogies are more than just a great way to make people laugh, they are a great way to show people that you care. You want to make analogies that compare the current situation to one that the audience is familiar with. For instance, if you know someone's favourite show, making analogies to that show creates closeness with that person. It shows you know what they like and are actively thinking about it. Even more powerful is to relate the current event to a different event that you and the audience were both a part of. For instance, if you're watching a movie where a guy is stabbed and bleeding: "This is just like that time at the company retreat when Paul spilled ketchup all over himself." The beauty of analogies is that the example doesn't have to be funny in its own right; instead it's the unexpected familiarity is what makes it funny.

It's a difficult skill to learn, but here's how you practice. Every time a non-typical event happens (something drops to the floor, someone says something weird) think of related events. Did someone else do this in a memorable setting? Is there a famous instance of this? What or who is similar to this, and why. It's going to take some time at first. It will be slow. But the more you practice, the quicker they'll be at your fingertips.

Here are a few examples:

Situation: A coworker is in a meeting acting a little too big for his britches

To coworker: I haven't been paying attention, when did Jack get replaced by Dwight Schrute?

Situation: You're in line behind someone whose pants are sagging and showing their asscrack.

You identify the most well known reference: Plumbers.

To Partner: That reminds me, we need to fix the sink.

The analogy doesn't have to be the most brilliant thing ever, but it has to click with your audience. The more unexpected the reference, the better. Knowing your audience makes all the difference.

Practice, practice, practice!

Parody: Parody is the act of imitating to be someone else for the sake of mockery. This can be anything from impressions of celebrities to acting like the bus driver in a story to your friends. People like seeing someone act like a person they know and mimic their essence. It makes us giddy for whatever reason. There's nothing really deep or difficult about it, if I put on a voice like your mom and say things your mom said, you're probably going to laugh.

Satire: Satire is probably the most misunderstood form of humor going, partly because the definition is a bit vague.

From the Oxford Dictionary: [satire is] the use of humor, irony, exaggeration, or ridicule to expose and criticize people's stupidity or vices, particularly in the context of contemporary politics and other topical issues.

That covers pretty much everything from Shakespeare to TikTok videos. Do yourself a favor – don't worry about Satire. It's not a super useful technique for your day-to-day life, and if you start describing what you're doing as satire, people will start describing you as a douche.

Now this isn't a complete list of tools by any means, but it should give you a window into the most common reasons people laugh. Hopefully you can use these to begin to identify why things are funny, with the end goal of harnessing that and using it to your advantage.

Chapter 2 - Identifying Funny

The next step to becoming a funny person is to take the techniques that we just learned about and use them to dissect things that we find funny. Whenever you see or hear something that you think is funny, no matter how small it is, try to understand why. Focus particularly on real life situations and less on TV and movies because real life situations are much easier to emulate. Scripted situations are difficult because the context is often carefully constructed. In fact, your first step to determining why something is funny should always be *understanding the context.*

2.1 Context

I can't stress this enough: context is the main thing you need to think of when trying to make someone laugh. Comedy is chaotically subjective. A person's sense of humor is as unique as their personality; it's based not just on their physiology, but also on their life experience. What a person has seen and heard and felt warps their sense of humor. Understanding the context of a joke and being able to quickly assess what needs to be known to get a joke and the emotional slant required of the audience to appreciate the humor are paramount to becoming a universally funny person. Beyond that, context is the tool you need to be able to quickly and precisely craft jokes that connect with your audience. As such, we need to have a full understanding of how context works. There are a few levels to this:

- **Literal**: Someone can only get a joke if they know what you're talking about. Like we mentioned earlier, you wouldn't get the joke about hunters if you had never heard of hunting before. The same is true of every funny thing. When you find something funny, the first thing you should do is think to yourself: "What did I need to know to find that funny." If I grew up in another part of the world would I get it? If I was a different gender/race/age/etc would I find this funny?

  This is also important for things that people find funny that you just don't get. Is there something in the context that you are unfamiliar with? Research and figure out what would have had to be different for you in order to get that joke. This understanding of context is crucial for being able to connect with whatever audience you're speaking with.

- **Emotional**: Emotional context is arguably more important and unarguably more difficult to understand than literal context. Emotional context involves knowing a person's feelings and beliefs. A lot of people hold certain things sacred depending on their own personal experience, and those feelings will change what they find funny. It doesn't matter how funny your joke about religion is, someone who thinks it's morally wrong to mock the Lord isn't going to laugh. The more you can understand the feelings of a person, the more you're able to tune into their humor.

When you examine something that makes you laugh, consider your emotional context. Do you only find that funny because you hold certain beliefs? There are jokes that conservatives laugh at that liberals don't, because of their emotional context. There are certain biases that you have that cloud your own judgement of funny, and until you are aware of those it becomes impossible to be impartial towards humour.

–   **External:** External context is what is going on around you. Obviously, the type of humor you are going to present depends very much on your surroundings. If you're at a funeral, you joke differently than if you are at a bar. When you're analyzing something that makes you laugh, you have to step back and be sure that it isn't just funny **in that setting**. This is the *"you had to be there"* effect. There is a lot more that goes into something being funny than just the words or actions, it's also everything else around. To fully understand why something is funny you must take in all the variables. Were we having some drinks? Was I overtired? Was there a relief from something that heightened the laughs? It's important to objectively look at why something is making you laugh. Just because you're laughing doesn't mean other people will also. You must factor in everything going on in the moment to be able to fully assess the humor of a situation/

Understanding the context of both yourself and your environment is crucial to understanding why something is funny.

Train your Brain
An exercise in context

Context is such a powerful tool that it can completely control whether or not something is funny. In fact, a common idea parroted by comedians is that *anything can be funny*. It's often misunderstood by the general public to mean that nothing is sacred to comedians, but what it actually means is that if you find the right **context**, anything can be funny. If you find the proper angle and the proper audience there can always be humor. For instance, to me there is nothing funny about breast cancer, but I've heard breast cancer survivors make great jokes about it, especially to other survivors.

In this exercise you'll be given non-funny ideas and you need to find a **context** in which these could be funny. I'll give you an example:

A baby cries uncontrollably

It's not an inherently funny situation. You don't see a baby crying uncontrollably and laugh at it. But is there a situation in which it could be funny? Try to think outside the box a bit, and let go of realism. It's like working backwards – you have the punchline, what is the set up that makes it funny? My approach is to think of a reason that a baby would be crying that would be funny. There isn't a lot of real reasons, since babies mostly cry at sad things, but what if the baby was crying for a grown up reason? What if the baby deserves to be crying? From there I can come up with this.

A baby cries uncontrollably on the television. Below reads the headline:
FBI thwarts Evil billionaire baby's genocidal plan for world domination thwarted

Now it's a bit funny. The baby is now crying because he

didn't get to commit a genocide, which is much funnier than if it was hungry. You have to think outside the box to come up with a premise that not only justifies the unfunny thing, but makes us happy to see it.

Now you try it.

Situation: **An old woman falls**

Situation: **A school bus crashes**

Situation: **The world explodes**

By unlocking the understanding of why *everything can be funny* you open yourself up to a world of jokes. If everything is funny then all you need to do is discover the context. Context is one of the fundamental pillars of understanding funny, and the more you can master it the funnier you will be.

2.2 Understanding Funny: Examples

Once you understand the context for why something is funny, examine exactly how it is funny. Anytime you or someone else laughs at something, try to figure out why. Were you caught off guard? Was there a release of tension? Were you led to believe one thing and then had your expectations subverted? Was there a clever twist that made you grin? Maybe you were just uncomfortable and didn't know what else to do?

It's not always easy to pick out what is happening, especially because there is usually a combination of factors at play. Let's go through a few examples that most people are familiar with and analyze why they are funny:

Mime: Chances are good you don't find mime's funny, Lord knows I don't. Dancing around in their pyjamas with their smug faces. But they've been around since ancient Greece and you know what they are, so there has to be some sort of appeal, right? Plus, secretly we all kind of like Mr. Bean, and he's the same schtick. Mime is a good study into how lowering the contextual bar for understanding allows you to cast a wide net with your appeal. Let's break it down.

> **Context** – If you're going to be around for an artform for millennia, you must have a universally understood context. This is one of the secrets of the appeal of mimes – everyone gets them. By not speaking they don't alienate anyone. No matter where you're from in the world, you understand a mime's language. Beyond that, mimes tend to deal with very easy to understand themes. They're either pulling a rope, or stuck in a box, or eating a piece of fruit that isn't there.
> Comedy is a numbers game, no matter how funny you are, you'll only ever make a certain percentage of people laugh. So, while mimes may not have a huge percentage of people who laugh at them, by making themselves accessible to everyone they are able to find the people

who enjoy their art. It's part of the reason that foreign films often don't have a huge appeal in North America. Sure, they could be amazing, but a whole chunk of us refuse to read subtitles. So, the easily accessible context works hugely in mime's favor.

Silliness – There's no denying the playful silliness of a mime. It seems funny as a kid, and sort of creepy as an adult. But the facial expressions, outfits, and actions are all the kind of goofiness that puts us at ease and opens us up to laughter. How can't he get out of that box? It's not even there!

Expectation – Part of the reasoning behind the silly outfit is more than to get laughs, it's to let the audience know that this is supposed to be funny. The outfit sends signals to anyone watching that this isn't insanity, this is planned. If a dude in jeans and a t-shirt started acting as though he was stuck in a box you might be concerned for his mental health or interested in his drugs, but a mime sets us up for the joke.

Surprise – many of the individual gags that a mime will do are based on surprise. The mime is just walking along and then suddenly he runs into something that's not even there! Oh, it's a wall. It's a real treat the first time you see it. Obviously for most of us it's so old hat that the surprise has faded, but if you watch a child or child-like person watch a mime you can see the surprise on their faces.

Repetition – He's in that goddam box forever. Eventually it takes so long that it gets ridiculous, and you can't help but laugh.

Timing – If you've ever seen a good mime you'll have to concede that they have an excellent sense of timing. A mime knows how long to hold a gag to get as much as they can, even if it's not much. They often know exactly when to move on or when to start something new, which can really only be perfected through hours of practice. There's no shortcut on this one.

External Factors: Anytime I've seen a mime absolutely dazzle a crowd it's been during a nice summer day in a park in a tourist district. The crowd is on vacation and are happy to see anything. I've never seen a mime get a laugh on Tuesday at 10 am in the financial district. Don't underestimate this.

Sitcoms: Sitcoms dominated television for decades, and although they are starting to die out, they have been extremely influential on humor and how people interact. People born before YouTube have the dialogue patterns from sitcoms ingrained in them, so being able to understand how the humor works helps you to relate. Sitcom dialogue is an excellent study of cleverness and can give you a great window into the importance of setups when trying to appear clever.

- **Context** – If you watch the pilot episode for any sitcom, the majority of the time is spent setting up context. They have to introduce to everyone and explain the world in which the show takes place. The higher concept the show is, the more background you have to explain. The concept the sitcom 3rd Rock From the Sun is: *aliens from another galaxy have come on a research mission to earth to study humans.* That takes more time to explain than the concept of the Friends, which is: *these people are friends.* By choosing a broad appeal that requires very little extra context, shows like Friends and The Office can be instantly understood by most people around the world.

- **Familiarity/Likeability** – By showing the same people in the same setting every week the audience becomes familiar with the cast and surroundings, and watching becomes a thing of comfort. There isn't any work getting to know context, we know these people and can dive right in. At the same time, the show is designed to make us like the characters. This likeability makes us much more likely to find them funny, and also aids in creating tension.

- **Repetition** – If something gets a huge laugh in a sitcom, you can bet your sweet ass you're going to see it again. Jokes are retold in different words over and over again, and catchphrases are used without shame. Especially before the internet, you could repeat everything and as long as it was in a slightly different package it was fine. Also, because people have watched the previous episodes, references to previous funny moments are sprinkled in as a little treat.

- **Tension/Expectation** – Sitcom is short for situation comedy, and that is a clue to where most of the humor is derived from. Generally, each episode of a sitcom features several different plot lines revolving around situations that need to be resolved. Jerry accidentally agrees to wear the puffy shirt and has to find a way out of it. Joey pretends he owns a Porsche and gets too deep into the lie and has to get out. Because we like these characters, we are emotionally invested in the resolution. As the tension builds, we feel that, and the sitcom exploits that to get laughs. By continually building and releasing the tension, they are able to control our emotions. Also, because we know the characters, we know how they will respond in situations. So because of our expectations, that tension is even easier to build because we have pre-existing context.

- **Cleverness (dialogue)** – Although the situations drive the show and are the overall vehicle for humor, the real laugh producer in most sitcoms is witty dialogue. In some sitcoms it seems like every second line is a witty response. Like here is a typical exchange from Friends:

Joey: Tell him Joey Tribbiani says hello... he'll know what it means.

Chander: You sure he's going to be able to crack that code?

Chandler uses irony to point out that what Joey said is stupid, which we enjoy because Joey is a little smug in his perceived use of code. If you were unfamiliar with the show and didn't already know that Joey is stupid and Chandler is clever and funny you might not get this, because I can think of a lot of contexts where that makes sense. Say Joey Tribbiani is a mob boss of some sort, telling someone he says hello could be a threat of some sort, and saying "he'll know what it means" would make sense. But because of the context, we know that it's Chandler delivering the burn.

The joke is fine, but the real thing to learn from sitcom cleverness is the art of the set up. Sitcom conversations are kind of like pro wrestling matches – all parties are working together to entertain. And like wrestling, the loser is sometimes doing the most work. Sitcom jokes are so perfect because the set ups are beautifully worded. Like the one above from Joey; no one would ever talk like that. You'd just say *"Tell him Joey Tribbiani says Hello"*, but that doesn't open up Chandler for a witty comeback.

As we mentioned earlier, the hard work is in the setup. In this case, Joey is setting up Chandler by using wording that is slightly off from normal. If we look at this example from Seinfeld, we can see an added twist where Jerry adds an extra element to create a setup for himself **(context – Jerry has just received a spam phone call. Also, at this time in history people still had phones nailed to the wall in their homes and not cell phones on their person):**

Jerry: "This isn't a good time."
Telemarketer: "When would be a good time to call back, sir?"

Jerry: "I have an idea, why don't you give me your home number and I'll call you back later?"
Telemarketer: "Umm, we're not allowed to do that."
Jerry: "Oh, I guess because you don't want strangers calling you at home. Well, now you know how I feel."

You can see that by asking a leading question, Jerry is able to set himself up for a great joke. The joke itself is pretty straightforward, pointing out the telemarketers obliviousness to the annoyance he is calling and pointing it out in a beautiful way. Jerry could have responded to *"When would be a good time to call back, sir"* by directly saying "Do you realize how annoying this is? Never call me back" and gotten the same point across in a much less funny way. But instead, Jerry wants to use misdirection to surprise the telemarketer. He asks the question in a very innocent, earnest tone, which leads the telemarketer to believe that Jerry is trying to be helpful. This setup of expectation is important, because it creates the surprise when Jerry comes back with his point.

The key is that Jerry isn't asking the question to get information – he already knows the answer. In fact, he's counting on it. Instead, he's manipulating expectation to camouflage his punchline, thus adding to the surprise. Remember how important surprise is to comedy. By looking a step ahead, and creating the setup himself, Jerry is able to deliver a substantially stronger joke than he could have by jumping right to the punchline.

- **Cleverness (Plot)** – Beyond the cleverness at the micro level of dialogue, sitcoms also used cleverness in the plot structure. As I mentioned above, the driving force of the shows is the outrageous yet relatable situations that we see portrayed. This is a form of cleverness on its own, as it's difficult to continually dream up these type of interesting ideas. But beyond that, almost every sitcom episode revolves around multiple situations. Usually several characters will be caught up in one plot while the remaining characters are up to something totally different. The cleverest of sitcoms will find unexpected ways for these two plots to become intertwined. The cleverness is in taking several stories that seem grossly unrelated and finding a believable way for them to cross. If it's too predictable or too insane it doesn't register as clever with the viewer, but when it's done just right it creates a sense of joy and wonder and people react as though they've seen a magic trick.

- **Timing** – because sitcoms are planned out, both dialogue and actions always happen with impeccable timing. There's always the perfect break in conversation to say the snappy line, the wrong person always walks in at just the wrong time to make the situation funny, and people having an affair are always caught mid-act. Everything is always geared to have the absolute perfect timing. Ironically, it's potentially the undoing of sitcoms. Because real life is never so perfectly timed, sitcoms feel incredibly fake, and eventually, people got sick of them.

- **Misc:** On top of everything listed here, many sitcoms also made use of a laugh track. This exploits a very simple truth about comedy: laughter is contagious. Hearing other people laugh triggers it in you, for a couple of reasons. First of all, as humans, we want to be a part of the group. If everyone is laughing, we instinctually don't want to be the only one left out. Also, hearing others laugh instantly assures us that what we heard was a joke. It strengthens the context of this being a funny moment and relaxes the listener. If you watch a clip of a sitcom without the laugh track it appears as though a bunch of psychopaths are having a conversation. Never underestimate the power of group laughter.

Mull it over
Friends vs Seinfeld

On the surface, *Friends* and *Seinfeld* seem like pretty similar shows. The premise and setting are almost identical. In fact, most of the joke mechanics are the same too. But the **tone** is very different. Understanding the tone that your audience enjoys can tell you a lot about what they'll laugh at.

Friends: While the characters may tease each other, the overall tone is positive. Some characters attack (Chandler), but overall the group is uplifting. They want to help, and the humor comes from helping each other overcome obstacles.

Seinfeld: Almost all of the jokes are attacking something. Anyone too nice is to be mocked. The humor comes from characters getting their comeuppance because of their selfish deeds.

If someone prefers *Friends* then they're likely to prefer jokes with an optimistic slant. *Seinfeld* fans are more likely to prefer a cynical take.

Understanding someone's sense of humor is more than just mechanics, tone is everything!

Improv: The best thing about going to an improv show is that it's one of the few times in life where you could probably beat up everyone in the room. Improv may have all of the pretension of jazz with none of the coolness, but when it's done well it is incredible. Unfortunately it doesn't translate very well to video (aside from *Who's Line is it Anyway?*), but you'd be hard pressed to find a live crowd that doesn't enjoy it. Improv performers do an excellent job of exploiting shared context to make moments. Let's see how:

- **Context**: One of the things that makes improv connect so strongly with live audiences is that the context is built as part of the show. If you've never seen improv, every scene begins with the performers asking the audience for suggestions. The requests are often leading ("Give me a profession"), but the answers are the foundation for the entertainment. This invites the audience to become part of the performance which subconsciously makes them more invested in the outcome. Because they have a hand in creating the scene, they are more interested in how it plays out. A good improv show feels almost as though the audience is part of the performance, and that creates an atmosphere of inclusiveness. By drawing people in and making them part of the show, they are more invested and more likely to laugh.

  The other contextual advantage to bringing the audience in on the creative process is the power of shared context. Because everything is created in the moment, only the people in the room are aware of the context. This creates the bond we mentioned, but it also creates a sense of fleetingness. Because this moment is a unique creation between performer and audience, it will never be duplicated. That temporariness causes it to feel more special and therefore the audience is more likely to appreciate it.

  These contextual advantages are all lost when improv is recorded and shown again, which is why it has never taken off on television or movies. It's a credit to the team at *Who's Line...* that they were able to make it work at all.

- **Cleverness** – the ability to create cohesive jokes off the top of your head is very impressive, and the audience at an improv show is aware of that. A big part of the reaction that improv gets is due to the appreciation of the audience for the quickness of the performers. And because the performers are well practiced in lateral thinking, they are able to use many of the techniques we've mentioned at a moment's notice.
Improv performers practice quite a bit to be able to do this kind of lateral thinking on the fly, it's not something that is inherent. The more you push yourself to use your brain in this manner, the easier it becomes to quickly think of clever responses under pressure.

- **Surprise** – As with any humor, surprise is a factor. Improv performers can only get laughs if they think of angles that the general audience hasn't thought of yet. By starting from the same place as the audience (the suggestions) the performer can beat the audience to any ideas, and therefore surprise them. Because the audience knows how little time the performers must prepare, they are more impressed with how fast the surprises come. This quick-fire continual surprise approach is a very well polished way to induce laughter.

- **Repetition** – A good improv troop will always bring back jokes and references to things that happened earlier in the show. Why stop at one laugh when you can get two for the same amount of work? Keep an eye out and see how often you see things repeated.

- **External Factors** – 15 years of live comedy performance have taught me that the atmosphere in the room plays a huge role in how people enjoy the show. 15 people watching an improv show in a huge, bright, hot room are not going to laugh the same way that 150 people crammed in a small dark room will. Being surrounded by laughter and feeling anonymous in the dark crowd simply allows people to laugh more. Even in this professional setting, external factors can sometimes be the most influential thing.

Twitter: Twitter might be a dying platform, but for a solid decade it was the go-to place to find funny takes on current events. It's difficult to be funny in text, and even more difficult to do so with a character limit, but some people have absolutely nailed it. In contrast to most humor, a lot of the laughs from twitter come from cleverness rather than surprise. If it is something shocking, it's usually absurd as opposed to unexpected. It's difficult to get the same kind of shock value through words alone, so another approach is often needed. And with Twitter's character limit, people have to work hard to get their point across in limited space, requiring more cleverness. Let's take a look at a few examples of popular funny tweets to see what the big deal is:

The first example is one of a very clever self-contained joke that doesn't require a lot of context. That relatability means that almost everyone can get the joke, so it has a solid mass appeal. The humor is derived mainly from a clever observation.

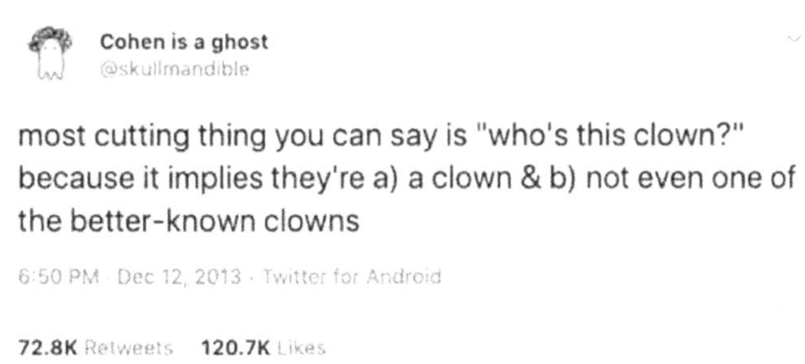

- **Context:** You need to know that there have only been a couple of famous clowns in recent history, and that "Who's this clown?" is an oft-used expression.

- **Hyperbole:** After reading the full tweet, still no one believes that it is the most cutting insult imaginable. The writer knows that, but is using hyperbole to manage expectations.

- **Expectation/Suspense:** By starting with "most cutting thing you can say" the tweet gears the reader to expect something obviously hurtful, so "who's that clown" is subverting that right away and putting the reader off balance. Then by breaking the punchline into two parts and having a) be very obvious, we build suspense with the reader as they know b) has to be the joke. And of course, b delivers the unexpected surprise twist.

- **Cleverness:** The tweet has some subtle cleverness–which is that is the extra layer of insult unintentionally added to "who is this clown". By realizing that there are only a handful of well-known clowns, the reader has logically deduced that any clown you don't know must be pretty unsuccessful. Then they simply pointed that out to us in a well worded way.

The next example is of the absurd variety that we talked about earlier. There isn't any clever observation here, but instead the surprise of the whimsy drives the humor.

- **Context:** You have to know what NASA is, and that they

sent astronauts to the moon. You also have to be familiar enough with Twitter to know that fake, conceptualized hypothetical conversations are commonplace. If you'd never seen the format, it would probably be a bit confusing. Also, you'd have to know that we haven't been to the moon that often and there's lots of it we can't see, so it sort of seems like there's lots we don't know about it.

- **Surprise:** Each line of the tweet is a jump up in silliness, and its that unexpected nature of each part that keeps us entertained. Even the set ups are designed to catch us off guard. The first line is NASA being surprised that the astronauts are back early, which is slightly amusing because we all know astronauts aren't doing anything without ground control being aware. Certainly not returning to earth. On top of catching us off guard, this also lets us know that it is a joke that we are reading, and we shouldn't take it seriously.
The next line is the obvious surprise, and most likely the thought that the whole tweet was based upon. *Moon's haunted.* We all know it isn't, so hearing it is a surprise, but the wording does more than just get the information across. It also tells us that the haunting is threatening, and that the astronaut doesn't have time to explain.

  NASA's response isn't a huge surprise, but it is very different than how we expect NASA to speak. Then the last line then shocks us again. We would expect the astronauts to simply be returning to earth to escape the haunting, but instead they subvert expectations by grabbing a gun and heading back to fight. The continuous build of these surprises is satisfying and keeps us entertained.

- **Cleverness:** Most of the cleverness in the tweet is in the wording. It's designed to manage expectation and surprise brilliantly, all while keeping a light tone. The additional detail of making the gun a pistol (a very small weapon to have returned all the way to earth to get) adds an extra element of absurdity which surprises and pleases our brains. These little details transform the idea from kind of funny to brilliant.

Books: Let's just be straight up honest: almost nobody laughs out loud while reading a book. You're never on the bus and hear someone laughing only to turn around and see them holding a tattered novel, and if you did, you'd assume they were a lunatic. That's not to say that books aren't funny, but their solitary nature tends to stifle laughter. Now, lumping all of literature into a single category is a bit flippant, but realistically you're probably not planning to write a hilarious novel. Learning to be funny in this format isn't the most useful, but having some sense of how to be funny in print is important. So what we want to glean from this is a general sense of the tools that writers use to make books funny. If you're a literature snob, don't send me an email.

- **Context:** The beauty of books is that they have an enormous amount of time to create context. Sometimes non-fiction books will demand some background knowledge, but fiction books are self contained universes. All you need to know is within those pages, so authors are free to create worlds that can be inherently funny in their absurdity. This shared context between the author and the reader can draw the reader into the world and create a fertile ground for humor.

- **Cleverness:** I think it's undeniable that the funniest books are fraught with cleverness. It's much more difficult to surprise or shock in print, and all tone and presentation is lost, so cleverness is the main source of humor available. This can take many forms. In a micro sense, the way that sentences are constructed can be clever (similar to how we examined Tweets) and self-contained jokes can be made. Like sitcoms, dialogue can be carefully choreographed to ensure clever retorts and timing. But beyond that, there is often a macro form of cleverness in books. There is sometimes an overarching satirical theme where the book is trying to say something about today's society through a fictional world, like Orwell's *Animal Farm*. Oftentimes these overarching themes are cleverer than they are funny, and quite frankly this type of humor isn't going to come up much in day-to-day life. So, if this isn't your thing, don't worry about it.

- **Surprise/Expectation:** A lot of the surprise humor in books comes from creating strange and interesting worlds that amuse the reader in how quirky they are; think Douglas Adams' *Hitchhiker's Guide to the Galaxy*. The freedom of writing allows the writer to indulge their imaginations and create a universe full of surprises. Since the author creates the rules, they can keep the reader guessing, which keeps them entertained.

  In contrast, non-fiction books can surprise us with unexpected facts and stories. Biographies can often be funny to the reader because they reveal facts about people that they think they know. Finding out that Meryl Streep* shit her pants once is funny, because we have a certain mental image of Meryl Streep. The expectation that comes with a public persona allows for easy surprise laughs, which is why late night talk shows lasted so long.

  *I have no idea if Meryl Streep ever shit her pants, I made that up.

Using these examples as a guide you can break down anything that people find funny and understand why it makes them laugh. Context and expectation are usually the two biggest driving forces and the ones that you should pay the most attention. Learning to use context to manipulate expectation is what allows you to start to control humor and change an interesting thought into one that makes people laugh.

Train your Brain
Identify the funny for yourself

Now that you know what you're looking for, let's put your skills to the test. Here is another one of Reader's Digest top ranked jokes:

A turtle is crossing the road when he's mugged by two snails. When the police show up, they ask him what happened. The shaken turtle replies, "I don't know. It all happened so fast."

Why is this funny? Do as I've done with the previous examples to identify the context, as well as the techniques being used to elicit laughter. It's a short joke, but there is a lot going on in terms of silliness, cleverness, brevity, wording and surprise.

Chapter 3 - Creating Funny

By now you should have an idea how to break down funny moments and some idea how to understand what makes you laugh. Getting better takes a lot of practice. The more you put into it, the better you'll understand. You can't read a book on playing the violin and then play it without years of practice. Please continue to examine things that make you laugh so that you can better understand humor. But for us it's time to move on to how to use that knowledge to create funny moments. That is a much bigger challenge. It's one thing to be able to recognize what is happening; it's another thing altogether to create something for yourself.

Before you start reading this section, I want you to know it's going to be frustrating. You have to re-wire your approach so that you're thinking as a funny person does, and it's going to feel awkward and forced at first. There is a lot to think about here and you're not going to remember it all. I would suggest that you focus on a few of the techniques that really resonate with you, and work those at first. As you get more comfortable, you'll be able go back and practice other techniques.

Because it will take time to figure out which techniques and wordings work for your brain and your personality. In the world of stand-up comedy we call it *finding your voice,* and comedians say it takes at least 10 years to do so. In those 10 years you're trying out different angles and approaches, trying to find the one that works for you. It doesn't take that long in your real life because you're not trying to be professionally funny, but you'll still need to go through that process.

The way people see you is not always the way you see yourself, and the way that they receive your jokes is influenced by how they see you. Weirdly enough the journey towards becoming funny is a bit of a journey of self discovery. People's reaction to your jokes will tell you things about yourself that you didn't know. And until you truly know yourself you'll never be the funniest you can be.

However the process is a lot more fun and exciting than it seems. It doesn't take a lot of laughter to feel good, and the more you get the more you'll be encouraged to continue. Don't expect to be the life of the party immediately, be patient and give yourself a chance to learn. The laughs will come, and the reward is more than worth the effort.

With that said, let's get funny.

3.1 General Tips

Being able to recognize and understand funny are essential skills, but what we really want to do is take those concepts and start using them to create our own funny situations. When we set out to create a funny moment, there are three high level things that govern our success: **context, premise,** and **execution.** To make things easier, let's look at an analogy. It turns out that making someone laugh is surprisingly similar to making them dinner.

Context: If you're cooking dinner for someone and you want them to enjoy it, your chances of success are much higher if you know some things about them. You want to know what they like and dislike, what they're allergic too, and so on. If the person is a vegetarian, it doesn't matter how good the steak you made for them is, they aren't going to like it. The same goes for jokes. If the person thinks sexual humor is never ever funny, it doesn't matter how great your joke about anal sex is, they aren't going to laugh. Knowing the context of your audience is, as always, vital.

Context also applies to the external factors happening around you. Even if you make a mean hot soup, it isn't a great dinner if it's 40 degrees Celsius and your air conditioner is broken. A joke about a mothers-in-law isn't funny at your mother-in-law's funeral, regardless of how flawless the execution.

We've talked a lot about context, and we'll talk a lot more about it – it's that important.

Premise: The premise is what you're cooking for dinner. It's the raw ingredients that you're going to turn into a delicious dinner. In terms of making someone laugh, it's the concept that you think is funny that you want to share. If you're telling a story about the time you peed your pants at a wedding, the pants peeing is the premise. It's the main driving force behind why this thing is funny.

We didn't go over discovering the premise in the previous section because when it's properly executed, the premise may not be obvious. Because it's the starting point it can sometimes get obscured. For instance, in the sample joke we used, the premise is actually the fact that *check if they are dead* is an ambiguous phrase. That, more than likely, was the starting point and the joke was constructed around it. It's not necessary to know the premise to understand the laughs, but it is necessary for creating them.

Now, as we know, the better our ingredients, the easier it is to make a delicious meal. It's easier to make a $40 steak taste good than it is to make a $2 piece of liver. The more inherently funny your premise is, the easier it will be to make people laugh. You don't have to put in as much work to get the desired result. Imagine you're on your way to work and one of the following two things happens:

> 1) The bus stops quickly and you're thrown forward into a man wearing a monocle.

> 2) A monkey climbs in the window of the bus and steals a guys toupee, the guy starts chasing him around but his pants fall down and he trips and falls into a giant birthday cake, then the monkey puts on the wig and starts humping the guys face while an old lady faints.

You can tell both of those stories in a funny way, but the second one requires a lot less work to make funny. The first one you have to get into why in the hell is a guy rich enough to afford a monocle still riding the bus and try to find humor in the weird classism of it all, but the second one you just have to say what happened. The better your premise, the easier it is to get laughs.

Now, we all know that the best chefs in the world can make a delicious meal out of terrible ingredients. They can take food you don't like and prepare it so you wouldn't even notice. And in the same vein, the funniest people can take the worst premises and find the humor in them. But until you get that Michelin star, you want to try to work with the best premises possible. Remember that no matter how good the premise is, if it doesn't match with the context of your audience, it's all for not. But in general, a great premise can make up for weaker context. The better you can get at choosing your premises, the easier the process will become.

Execution: The execution is all about how you cook up those raw ingredients. High quality ingredients require less preparation than lower quality ones. But the execution is all about doing the best you can with whatever you've got. Once you're committed to a meal all you can do is your absolute best to make it delicious. Same goes for jokes: once you've narrowed in on your premise, you want to present it in the best way possible.

For jokes, the execution is your ability to manage expectation, create surprise, and utilize the tools we've discussed to add flair. Adding hyperbole to your punchline is like adding chives to your mashed potatoes. They'd still be good without it, but it adds that extra touch. Execution is the slowest and most difficult step to learn, it takes practice and experience to know how to properly phrase things to maximize the laughs. And there's no *done.* Everyone can always get better at how they execute funny moments, so never stop learning.

By concentrating on context first and using that to filter through the premise and execution you can be sure that you're starting out from a point that the audience likes. If you're cooking dinner for someone who loves pasta more than anything, your pasta doesn't have to be as good as it would be if you cooked something they didn't like. I'll eat any burger, but I'll only eat the best fish. Jokes are the same. If you're joking about something that the audience already loves, your joke doesn't have to be as strong to get a laugh. To force them to laugh at something they don't enjoy takes a substantially stronger premise and execution. So focus on your audience and you'll find a shortcut to laughs.

Thinking Funny

There is one skill that I personally believe is most important for creating funny, especially on the fly, and that is **lateral thinking.** Lateral thinking is the backbone for pretty much any form of creativity and humor is no different. The idea is to think in different and creative ways to solve a problem. We've already practiced it a bit in our early exercise about context. By thinking about things in different ways, you can come up with different ideas. Seeing things in a different way than your audience is a very easy way to make things funny.

When you're thinking of jokes, you need to give yourself lots of options. Your first thought is unlikely to be the best available joke, so keep working on it. You sometimes will need to think of the perfect reference or wording or analogy, and the only way to do that is to come up with a lot of different possibilities. The fewer possibilities, the less chance that you'll find the optimal choice. This is how lateral thinking lets you be funnier. It essentially gives yourself more options and ideas for each situation, which lets you be funnier more often. Also, the less creative you are, the more likely you are to start repeating yourself. Telling the same jokes over and over again is a trap that many people find themselves falling into. Your creative thinking ability will determine your ceiling as a funny person, so it's up to you to develop it. Push yourself to see new angles and create new jokes, even just in thought. This will help you broaden your horizons and ultimately become a funnier person.

Train Your Brain
Think laterally, stupid!

As a kid I loved brainteasers. I loved that you had to approach them in a different way in order to understand them. The answer was always right there, but you just had to think differently to get it. Try out these brainteasers. None of them are difficult, but they all require a different approach to thinking. The trick is to come at the problem in as many different ways until you find one that feels right.

1. There is a man who lives on the top floor of a very tall building. Everyday he gets the elevator down to the ground floor to leave the building to go to work. Upon returning from work though, he can only travel halfway up in the lift and has to walk the rest of the way unless it's raining! Why?

2. A man and his son are in a car accident. The father dies on the scene, but the child is rushed to the hospital. When he arrives the surgeon says, "I can't operate on this boy, he is my son! " How can this be?

3. A man is wearing black. Black shoes, socks, trousers, coat, gloves, and ski mask. He is walking down a back street with all the streetlamps off. A black car is coming towards him with its light off but somehow manages to stop in time. How did the driver see the man?

4. One day Kerry celebrated her birthday. Two days later her older twin brother, Terry, celebrated his birthday. How?

5. A man died and went to Heaven. There were thousands of other people there. They were all naked and all looked as they did at the age of 21. He looked around to see if there was anyone he recognized. He saw a couple and he knew immediately that they were Adam and Eve. How

did he know?

6. A murderer is condemned to death. He has to choose between three rooms. The first is full of raging fires, the second is full of assassins with loaded guns, and the third is full of lions that haven't eaten in 3 years. Which room is safest for him?

7. There are two plastic jugs filled with water. How could you put all of this water into a barrel, without using the jugs or any dividers, and still tell which water came from which jug?

8. What is black when you buy it, red when you use it, and gray when you throw it away?

9. This is an unusual paragraph. I'm curious how quickly you can find out what is so unusual about it. It looks so plain you would think nothing was wrong with it. In fact, nothing is wrong with it! It is unusual though. Study it, and think about it, but you still may not find anything odd. But if you work at it a bit, you might find out

Answers:

1. He's a very short man and can only reach the halfway button. On rainy days he has an umbrella
2. The surgeon is the child's mother
3. It's daylight
4. The older brother is a twin, but not Kerry's twin
5. No bellybuttons
6. 3 – after years the lions would be dead
7. Freeze the water
8. Charcoal
9. It doesn't contain the letter 'e'

3.2 Jokes

Up until this point I've been casually referring to jokes, because I think we all recognize a joke when we hear one. At least a good joke. But when it comes time to sit down and craft one, it gets a little muddier. Especially because for a lot of us, our idea of what a joke is can be a little antiquated. A lot of us hear jokes and we picture an old timey *knock-knock* or *why did the chicken cross the road* sort of thing. But for the sake of this book, we'll define a joke as anything designed to make people laugh. However, in order for it to be a **good joke**, there has to be a certain *something*. There has to be a leap in logic that causes the listener to see the subject in a different light. This is the thing you "get" when you "get a joke". Without this connection, the joke is meaningless and random. Let's look back at the rule of three for a moment to try to clarify.

As mentioned, the biggest factor in eliciting laughter is surprise. Remember that the rule of three works by establishing a pattern to create expectation in the listener, and then breaking it to surprise them. So, based on that, I should be able to say anything as the third item and have it be funny. But that is not the case. For instance, if I was to say:

> *My three favourite days of the year are my Thanksgiving, Christmas, and Fart Sandwich.*

The listener is more confused than entertained. Because there is no logical leap between other holidays and fart sandwich. The listener is surprised, sure, but there's no satisfaction in it. There's no aha moment to give the audience that rush of "getting it". A good joke leaves the audience pleasantly surprised, not confused. It's a big part of the reason why randomness isn't as funny as we expect it to be, it lacks that logical connection. It's possible to make people laugh without this connection. If you watch Chris Farely's legendary entrance to the Late Show with David Letterman, you'll see tons of laughs without any connection. But that kind of comedy is inherently risky and difficult. To be consistently, universally funny you need to understand how to create solid jokes with a logical leap that isn't too far for the audience to come along but is far enough to create that sense of satisfaction from "getting it".

I know that's absurdly vague, but I don't want to discourage creativity. In general, most jokes take the form of a setup and a punchline. The setup is designed to make the audience think in a certain way. It usually involves some misdirection to manage expectations. Then the punchline is the surprise at the end. The punchline takes what the setup did to the audience's mind and uses that information to surprise and amuse. There's usually a twist of some sort that catches the audience of guard, and that's what evokes laughter.

Comedians will tell you that the best jokes contain as few words as possible, they just get right to the meat. And there's no better example than the cliché by this point but still brilliant Henny Youngman classic: *Take my wife, please.* It's a complete joke in only four words. The setup is *take my wife.* To be fair, there is a little bit of context needed here. Back when people actually talked to each other, *Take my wife* was often used to segue into talking about your wife. *Take my wife for example, she's an excellent cook.* So when people back in the 50's heard *take my wife,* they expected it to be followed by some information about his wife. Youngman has manipulated the expectations of his audience, so then *please* is completely out of left field. Notice how it completely changes the meaning of the setup. This twist is what tricks the brain into laughing at jokes.

There is no right or wrong way to make jokes, but you want to keep in mind expectation and surprise, as these are the key tools when it comes to jokes. No matter what the subject matter, the mechanisms behind what makes jokes work are the same. If you can understand how to manage expectation and surprise, you can make funny jokes out of just about anything.

Setups

Learning how to build funny moments and stories is an art, and while the punchline is what sparks the laughs, the hard work is done behind the scenes. It's like a movie – the actors get the credit but 90% of the work is done behind the scenes. Learning to lay the foundations for funny moments is what leads to consistent punchlines. Very rarely does the perfect setup come along organically, most often it must be cultivated. You need to latch onto funny ideas and word questions in ways that stimulate set ups.

Look at old vaudeville duos – there is always one guy getting all the laughs. But the other guy, the *straight man*, as they are called, is the one who does all the work. It's the wording of the setup that allows for jokes to flow so freely. This is the real art. Because every setup is a new idea, and the punchline is built on that idea. Coming up with new ideas is hard, but building on them is easy.

The setup for the joke should have all of the information needed to get the punchline, but doesn't give away the twist. A good setup has *only* the information needed to get the joke. The setup is used to prime the audience's expectations so that the punchline can surprise them and get a laugh. In practice, you'll need to master two different kinds of setups: setups for yourself, and setups for others.

Setups for yourself are straightforward. You're going to deliver the punchline, so you know all of the information needed to get the joke. Here's an example:

> *I had a real scare last night – I found a lump on my testicle. Scared the life out of me. Luckily it was a skittle.*

You get to frame the setup however you want to trick people into feeling what you want. In this case, sympathy plus a little bit of a scare. Then the punchline twists it and provides the relief.

Setups for others is a little more complicated. The goal here is to give the other person the chance to bring a funny twist. The better you know someone, the easier this is. Some easy examples of this are callbacks, which we'll discuss in detail next. If your friend had a funny name in college, simply asking about it in front of a new audience serves the purpose.

> *Hey Steve, what did they used to call you in college?*

There's nothing funny in what you said, but it gives Steve the opportunity to repeat a funny thing. Another method is bringing up something that you know the other person has a strong, funny opinion on. If you know someone hates Taylor Swift for some reason, you could set them up like this:

> *How much do you love that new Taylor Swift song?*

It gives them a chance to respond with something like:

> *I'd rather listen to my own mother's death rattle*

It takes time and practice to understand other funny people's rhythms, but once you do, you can make beautiful music together.

Far too often when people are trying to be funny, they become combative and defensive with other funny people, when the goal should be to work together to create funny moments. Funny conversations are like wrestling matches, both wrestlers working together creates the magic.

Tags

Sometimes when you tell a joke, there is an opportunity for what comedians call a *tag* (comedians in the UK call it a *topper,* but they also call pants *trousers* so let's not trust them). A tag is an extra joke that adds something to the previous punchline to get another laugh. They are incredibly useful for joking in a group of people, because it allows multiple people to be part of creating the joke. This shared context brings the group closer together and creates a strong bond.

Tags are also incredibly efficient at getting laughs because you don't need a new setup. Setups are the hard part of being funny, like I'll explain later. Tags allow you to get multiple laughs off the same setup, and because everyone is already laughing at the idea, they are much more likely to laugh at the tag. As such, the tags do not have to be nearly as strong a punchline as the original joke.

For instance, if your friend walks into a room full of people wearing an unexpected Hawaiian shirt, that serves as the setup to the joke. Assuming everyone present is familiar with Jimmy Buffett, you could probably get a laugh by saying *if it isn't the mayor of margarittaville!*

If that gets a big laugh, then I can almost guarantee that if someone else were to say *Well it's 5 o'clock somewhere!* will get a laugh too. A smaller one, but more than you'd expect, because everyone is still enjoying the first joke. You can see how much weaker the second punchline is, but because everyone already likes the premise they are inclined to continue to enjoy it. If you said the tag without the punchline, it doesn't have the same sort of impact.

There is a law of diminishing returns with tags, so be careful to not overtag a joke. Take note of when the laughter is dying off and pull the chute early. There's no sadder silence than that of being the last tag on a great joke.

Callback

A *callback* is a reference to a funny thing that happened previously. For instance, if you were walking with your friends and one of them was texting while walking and went headfirst into a pole, you'd probably all laugh (if they weren't badly hurt). And then if you were hanging out later and said something like "hey remember when Tim went face first into that light pole?", everyone will more than likely laugh again. Simply referencing the funny moment will do. However, a proper callback adds a joke instead of simply referencing the event. You'd get much bigger laugh if you saw that same friend sitting on the couch texting and you yelled dramatically "Tim, watch out for that pole!" This forces the group to make that logical leap of remembering Tim hit the pole, and that "getting it" causes them to laugh even harder. By indirectly calling back to that funny moment you add your own joke to an already funny moment, getting extra laughs.

Callbacks are a great way to get extra mileage out of funny moments. However, it's important to be keenly aware of context. You need to call back to a moment that the audience was a part of, but also that you're sure they will remember. There's nothing more awkward then a callback that no one gets. You have to make sure the event was big enough in people's memories that your indirect reference will be understood.

3.3 Key Concepts

Relating Funny

It's one thing to be able to recognize and understand funny, it's another big leap to be able to create funny things yourself. It's substantially easier to be a critic than a creator. It turns out that it's surprisingly difficult to explain a funny moment or idea in words to another human being. Think of it like drawing a picture – you could have that perfect image of what you want to draw in your mind, but your stupid fat hands are unable to properly convey your thought. The same is true of funny. You could have a perfectly hilarious idea in your head, but if you can't express it properly, no one else can enjoy it.

You must keep this in mind when you're trying to be funny. You have to try to put yourself in the head of the listener and focus on **context**.

Ask yourself:

Am I giving this person all of the backstory they need for this idea to be funny?

Does this person have the proper beliefs to find this idea funny?

Are this person's life experiences such that they will appreciate this?

Are there external factors that would make this inappropriate?

From what I know of this person's sense of humor, will they find this idea funny?

If you're confident that you've got the right audience for the idea, then you know that it's up to you to find the right medium to convey the idea. This is an excellent learning situation, because if you know the idea is funny and the context is there, then you know that if you don't get a laugh, it's because you didn't explain it properly. It happens to everyone, and if you analyze the situation, you should be able to figure out what went wrong. I know my friend's humor very well, but still sometimes I'll bring them an idea I *know* they'll find funny, but when I tell them, I get nothing. It's almost always because I forgot a vital piece of information, or I falsely assumed they knew something already, or I simply didn't convey the idea properly. But then I can step back and figure out what is missing, and I can correct it when I go to tell the idea to the next person.

So, if you have an idea that you just know is funny, and people aren't laughing at it, don't blame your sense of humor. It's most likely that you're not properly communicating the idea, which is no shame. It's a difficult skill that takes practice. Throughout this book I will give you tips for different situations on how to get your funny point across, and if you put in the work, you will notice a huge difference.

Here is a practical exercise that can help you work on wording funny ideas. I know that personally, I have a lot of self doubt. So, when my funny ideas don't get the response I expect, I used to turn inward and start to doubt my ability to decide what was funny. When I get like that, I use this exercise to get out of it. Take someone else's idea that you find really funny and try to put it into your own words. Take a bit of stand up, or some dialogue, or whatever really makes you laugh and try to take the essence of the idea and completely re-word it. Then tell the idea, in your own words, to other people and see what reaction is good. You know the idea is funny, so it's completely on you to get it across. Once I was able to re-tell people's ideas in a funny way, it gave me a huge leap forward in how to construct my own ideas.

Wording

A lot of the time you can get laughs off *how* you say something as opposed to *what* you say. The way you choose to word things can give you a huge leg up on everyone else. I've seen two people tell the same story and one be the life of the party while the other gets all but ignored. The proper description can make or break a funny moment, so don't be careless with your words. Try to take time to think about how you're going to phrase something before spitting it out.

There are a few simple tricks to get started. The first is the use of adjectives. It's a little thing, but if you can build yourself a mental thesaurus full of colorful adjectives that you can use to describe inanimate objects you can inject a little humor with almost no effort. Then you can use them almost like mad libs. The absurdity "Can you pass me that sloppy whore of a blanket" is more entertaining than simply asking for a blanket. The same can be done in other situations: "I had a real anal fissure of a day." It's like adding a bit of color to a picture, it spices it up.

Try to pepper your speech with some fewer known words as well, it keeps people on their toes. And I don't mean big words, don't make that mistake. Using big words people don't know makes you seem like a pompous turd, whereas using words like turd that people are familiar with but don't hear often makes people giggle. Keep your ears out for words that you like that are unusual and add them to your repertoire.

Mull it over
Hide the reveal

If you really want to be at the top of your game comedically, you need to get precise with your wording. It's not just about picking funny words, the other real secret to wording is in hiding the surprise. Ideally, you want to ensure that the audience can't fully get the joke until as late as possible. The perfect joke is not fully revealed until the final word. Here's an example from my stand up.

You know sex is fun because it's the only thing so fun that you'll do it even though sometimes it makes a baby. You'd never get on a roller coaster if occasionally at the end they handed you a kid.

You know sex is fun because it's the only thing so fun that you'll do it even though sometimes it makes a baby is the setup. It lets people know what I'm talking about.

You'd never get on a roller coaster if occasionally at the end they handed you a kid is the punchline.

Notice that *handed you a kid* is the last phrase. It isn't until the word kid that you can fully understand the idea. The surprise is last.

There is a real practical reason for this. As soon as the audience gets the joke, they want to laugh. But if you're still talking, they can't. The longer they have to hold their laughter, the less actual laughter there will be. Every instant you spend talking after the joke is a revealed is wasted laughter.

Whenever you want to deliver a joke, stop and work on your wording. Rearrange the sentence so that the reveal is at the very end.

Be Influenced

Keep your ears open for things that you find funny, and don't be afraid to allow things that you laugh at to influence how you make others laugh. Going even further, don't be afraid to imitate some of the things you find funny, especially as you begin this journey into being a funny person. You need to get used to the feel and the rhythm of saying funny things, and sometimes the best way to get your feet wet is by repeating some of the things you like.

I know this might seem against the whole point of learning how to be funny, but everyone learns by imitating at the start. Regardless of what you're doing, it's easiest to learn from what already exists and then build upon it, as opposed to trying to reinvent the wheel. Remember, you're not trying to become a legendary stand-up comedian, you're trying to become a funny person. The rules are different.

Know your punches

This is something that is super important in stand-up comedy, but it can be just as valuable to conversational skills. It's kind of hard to define exactly what a punchline is, but to me, it's the exact word or phrase that you say that you know when you say it, people are going to laugh. As we mentioned, ideally, they don't fully get what is funny until the last word, but sometimes it's the last several words. Regardless, you should know exactly when I say this, people will laugh. If you can't picture that exact moment, you need to work on your wording. To me the difference between a funny idea and a joke is that wording that induces laughter. I can look at my stories and tell you these exact moments.

This helps you not only build laughs, but also be more objective in your editing. If you know exactly where you expect people to laugh, you can keep track of whether they did or not. This gives you objective feedback into how funny the joke is. By paying attention to this and doing honest editing, you can start to be more consistently funny.

Listen to your Audience

There is no better advice that I can give to anyone than this: it's only funny if the audience laughs. Whoever it is that you're trying to entertain is the ultimate judge of funny. If you think it's funny and they aren't laughing than either you aren't explaining it properly or it's not funny to them. And if it's not funny to them, then in this moment, **it isn't funny.** The more you listen to the feedback from your audiences the more you will be able to recognize what does and doesn't work for you. It's hard to wrap your head around sometimes, but the world doesn't perceive you the way that you perceive yourself. If you don't consider how others see you, then you simply won't improve. Everyone fails when they're trying to be funny, the successful ones learn from it. The perennial failures are too stubborn. Be humble.

3.4 Types of Funny

With that said, let's create some funny. Before we get too far into it, let's define a couple more terms. It's convenient to classify funny in two different forms:

1) Reactively funny
2) Proactively funny

Let's define reactively funny as a joke or observation based on something that is going on around you. Making a joke about something that you see or hear, or any sort of response to outside stimuli. Your friend shows up in a ridiculous Hawaiian shirt and you say: *If it isn't the mayor of margarittaville* – you're being reactively funny. The set up is done for you, you just need to come up with the punchline. If you're going to be known as a funny person, this should be the focus of most of your efforts. This is how you appear clever and witty, and how you can adapt for all situations.

One of the benefits of reactive funny is that the context is built into the situation. Because you're joking about something that everyone has seen or heard, they are all well versed in the context of the situation. This is something that we mentioned earlier called **shared context** – you and the audience have both experienced the same thing, so you have a connection built on it. This is an incredibly strong tool for building likability and closeness.

Proactively funny on the other hand, requires you to construct the setup and the punchline. Examples of proactive funny are things like telling a story, physical humor, ice breakers, etc. Anything where there is no context, and you have to build it. For instance, when you're telling a story, you must tell enough backstory for the audience to understand what the hell you're talking about.

Proactive humor is difficult, but the advantage is that you can plan and practice your approach many times before employing it. With the proper discipline and self awareness you can ensure that your proactive funny attempts are solid before you set them free.

At first, you're going to have to force this mindset, and it's not going to be easy. Most times things aren't naturally funny, and it's frustrating to be searching for humor when it's not there. You're going to fail a lot at first. You're going to try to force things to be funny, and you're going to be wrong. Unfortunately, that's just how it works. You must fail a bunch before you're funny. But if you stick with it and train your brain to always be open and aware of funny, I promise you, it's worth it.

In the next chapters we will discuss both types of humor in details.

Chapter 4 - Reactively Funny

The true test of a funny person is the ability to make people laugh by using what is going on around them. The shared context as well as the spontaneity of making fun of your surroundings crystallizes people's vision of you as a funny person. If you're the kind of person who can give a funny response to any question, you're the kind of person people want to talk to. Any piece of news they'll take to you because they know you'll have an entertaining spin. Life Let's be frank, life can be boring and tedious, if you can make it interesting, people will notice.

The catch is that it's not easy. Creating jokes on the fly that are funny and relevant and then delivering them with the right timing is something that takes a lot of practice. What you're trying to do is a form of improv. If you're too young to remember *Who's Line is it Anyway?,* essentially a team of comedians create jokes and funny scenes off the top of their heads based on suggestions from the audience. It's very impressive to watch – it seems like they were born with this crazy ability. But the truth is: they practice. A lot. And weirdly. Google *improv practice* if you don't believe me. Try to resist the urge to bully these nerds. But it pays off. Reactionary funny is a skill like any other, and it can be learned.

It seems impossible at the outset, because you need to go through our three steps (context, premise, execution) in the blink of an eye, and deliver it with impeccable timing. It seems impossible to be able to do that consistently. And at first it might be impossible. At first you might need to take more time to think about the jokes, and by the time you're ready, the moment has passed. It may seem frustrating because you've put in all this effort to create a joke that will never be used. But the dirty little secret about improv and about reactionary funny in general is that it's a lot less off the top of their head than you'd think.

I've worked with many brilliant improv troupes and watched them perform night after night, and what you start to notice is that a lot of the suggestions are similar. The crowd in one town is likely to shout out the same suggestions as the town 20 miles down the road. There is a surprising amount of repetition. Maybe you won't see the exact same joke, but you'll see the same premise and the same context with a little twist. That happens in life too. If you think of a good joke for a situation and don't get a chance to use it, put it in your back pocket. Remember it. Chances are good you'll have another opportunity to use it, and you'll save time by having it at the ready.

Also, don't be afraid to re-use jokes, especially with a new audience. Look, the fact of the matter is this: great jokes aren't born every second. As you start your journey into funny, you'll hopefully notice that you think up more hits than misses. If you're under the delusion that everything you think of is hilarious, you're straight up wrong. So, when you *do* think of something that is genuinely hilarious, don't let it float off into the ether. Remember it and try to think of different situations/audiences that you can use it again. If you hang around a funny person long enough, you'll hear them repeat themselves. Don't make the mistake of thinking you're better than that.

Remember to that it's not a cardinal sin to repeat a funny thought you've heard elsewhere, especially when you're trying to get comfortable being funny. Try to take the essence of the idea and re-work it into your own words as opposed to straight parroting it, but trying on ideas that you *know* are funny is a good way to get your feet wet. It helps you work on your delivery. You know that the content is funny, so if it doesn't get laughs than you need to work on your presentation. There are no rules, and you're not trying to be a professional, you want to get comfortable and confident with making people laugh.

With that out of the way, let's get to the actual act of creating something funny. There is an art to noticing potential humor, and it's a lot different than analyzing things that make you laugh. Previously, we were looking at situations where the creating is done for us and breaking down why they made us laugh. In this case we want to look at a blank canvas and create funny on our own. We want to train our brains to look for potentially funny moments, but what are we looking for? What should you be focusing on to maximize comedy in every situation?

It's a complicated question with no simple answer, because there are a huge number of options. It's like if you were in a fight; you can't say exactly what to look for because you need to be on the lookout for a lot of different things. You need to be aware that he could punch with either hand, kick with either hand, grapple you, pull out a weapon, reveal he's a dinosaur in a human costume, whatever. You've got to take a similar approach to finding humor. Look at all the possibilities and see what is best for the situation. With that said, I'll walk you through some of the techniques that help me spot potentially funny moments in everyday situations.

4.1 Spot the Dog

The driving force of a huge chunk of reactionary comedy is identifying and communicating things that are out of place. It sounds ridiculously basic, but that's observational comedy in a nutshell. Jerry Seinfeld's billion-dollar empire is entirely based on pointing out things that are a little off. Here's what USA Today says is the best joke from his new Netflix special:

I go through customs and the guy asks me, 'Do you have any alcohol? Any drugs?' Is this an effective interrogation? Is anyone going, 'Bingo, you got me, I didn't see that question coming. 20 kilos right there.'

All he's doing is pointing out that this question is silly. It surprises people because they've heard it a million times but either never thought of it from this angle, or always thought of it from this angle and didn't think anyone else did. It's such a simple but powerful observation because it's very relatable. The execution is obviously top notch, but the seed that it grew from is pointing out something out of place. It seems so easy, but it takes time to be able to spot things that people will relate to. And it takes more time to learn how to express why they're out of place quickly and with surprise. What exactly are you looking for?

The ideal candidate is something that clearly doesn't belong but isn't immediately obvious to everyone. If you walk into a room and there are 4 lime green gorillas sitting around a table, you aren't the funny guy for pointing it out. Everyone notices that. You want to find the things that others miss. The more subtle the placement, the easier because simply by pointing it out you will make people laugh. If you can train yourself to notice things that are out of place, you can get a ton of easy laughs. In order to do so though, you have to learn to look in the margins. By that I mean pay attention to the things that you're not supposed to. While everyone is focused on the foreground of the picture, you look at the background. While everyone is listening to the woman on stage, you pay attention to the crowd. If someone is telling a story, check in on the little details. There's more likely to be something comically out of place in the fringes than in the focus.

For instance, take this picture:

If you only pay attention to the foreground, it seems pretty standard. But once you find the giant dog in the middle you get a little giggle. You want to be the person pointing out the dog. But you can only find the dog first if you're looking for it.

Hopefully you get the metaphor: the dog isn't always going to be a dog. The dog is sometimes going to be a misspelled word or a slip of the tongue. Sometimes the dog is a misprinted expiry date that says these canned tomatoes are good until 4/20/69. Anything that is out of place to the point that it will get a reaction from people, you want to be able to spot it immediately.

Once you've *spotted the dog*, that is your premise. That is the thing that is funny. Now you need to move on to the execution.

The secret to pointing something out to someone in the funniest way possible is that you don't want to tell them what's out of place. You want to guide them to find it for themselves. The surprise is much more effective if they notice it on their own. At its absolute most basic it can be literally pointing at a thing and forcing the audience to look at it. At the more advanced stages you'd make a joke that indirectly references the out of place thing which causes everyone to figure it out for themselves. While the more advanced route is usually funnier, the amount of effort you *need* to put into the execution to get a laugh is fully dependent on how inherently unusual the dog is that you're spotting. The more obviously funny, the less work you need to do. Conversely, the more obvious the out of place thing is, the quicker you need to point it out. Others will see it eventually, so you want to be first. When it's more subtle, you can take your time and find the perfect joke.

Think of these two examples:

1) A reserved friend who normally wears a t shirt and jeans walks into a party with a new brown fedora and leather jacket.

2) A reserved friend who normally wears a t shirt and jeans walks into a party shirtless with a giant dragon tattoo on his chest.

In the second situation you just need point this out to everyone ASAP. There's nothing you are going to say that is going to be as funny as them simply looking over and seeing that sight. Plus, if you don't point it out immediately, someone will beat you to it. Time is of the essence, so don't waste thought cycles on the execution. The second example, however, is a little more subtle. You can't just point at someone trying a new style and expect people to laugh. You know something is off, but you have to take the time to figure out what.

First, figure out the context. You're at a party, so your goal is likely to make the people around you laugh. This is your friend, so a lighthearted making fun of him is appropriate. The next step is a little tougher: what do the people at the party associate with fedoras and leather coats? If they're over 30 they likely think of Indiana Jones. If they're younger, they might think of a typical neck beard. If it's me at a party, it's likely full of 30+, so it would usually be Indiana Jones. Here is where you put in the extra work. Simply saying *you look like Indiana Jones* is exactly what you should avoid. That is telling them what is out of place. Instead, you want to elude to it, and let people figure it out for themselves. You want to make a reference to Indiana Jones that people will immediately get, and then they'll infer that he's dressed that way. Something like

> *Nice of you to take time out from raiding the lost ark to join us*

Or

> *Snakes! Why did it have to be snakes?!*

By referencing it indirectly you build the suspense as the audience tries to figure out what you're talking about. Then it adds to the delight when they figure it out on their own.

It takes a surprising amount of practice to be able to both identify things out of place and learn how to communicate. Start by simply pointing things out, but as you get more comfortable add layers to your observations so that people can figure them out for themselves.

The most important part is to always be observing. And as your observing, make jokes about what you see to yourself. Try to make yourself laugh. The more effort you put into thinking funny all the time, the easier it will be in those pressure situations when you need it. You want to be the first to see everything and the first to have their jokes ready about it. There's no shortcut unfortunately, only practice.

Train Your Brain
Learn to spot the dog

Noticing something out of place is a tough skill to learn, but the first step is to condition your brain to not just always be looking for the dog, but doing so as quickly as possible.

Here are some concepts to keep in mind. Commit these to memory and make them a habit.

1) **Check the background first** – everyone will be looking at the focal point, you want to scan the edges first. That's where the out of place things will be.
2) **Be vividly aware of context**. Many things are only out of place relative to what is going on. A *shout at the devil* t shirt isn't funny at a metal concert, but it is at a baptism.
3) **Go the extra mile**. Comedian Mitch Hedberg had a great joke about seeing someone throw a tomato at a band who stunk. It's a dated, but familiar image. He goes the extra mile to state: "who would bring a tomato to a concert?" In this case you can't spot the dog until you think about how the situation arose.
4) **Remove preconceived notions** – we accept a lot of things as normal, but if we set aside our biases they might actually be weird. This is why people from other cultures find so much of what we do strange – it's unfamiliar to them. Try to see things through an unbiased set of eyes.

4.2 That's Like the Time...

The absolute easiest way to make people laugh is to reference something that they've already laughed at. Once something is funny in your brain, thinking about it automatically makes you feel like laughing. There are entire friendships built on nothing but repeating lines from funny movies and shows. So knowing what your audience finds funny gives you a shortcut to making them laugh. By triggering them to recall funny memories, you start to become associated with funny in their heads.

This works for shows or movies that you know the audience enjoys (it is much more powerful if they are aware that you also enjoy the piece, as that shared context builds closeness), but it works even better for shared memories you have had with the person. Inside jokes, for lack of a better term. Any time you can organically reference a shared laugh you've had in the best you are almost guaranteed to have another giggle.

For example, there is a cashier at my local store that I see about once a week. I was next in line one day when an old man got in a big fight with him over change. The old man claimed he used a 20 dollar bill, while the cashier assured him it was a 10. They argued back and forth to the point that the manager had to be called and the video footage had to be checked, and sure enough, it was a 10. The man didn't apologize as much as he grunted acknowledgement and then left. I was next to the cashier and I joked about what happened (the release of tension aids this) and I went on my way. The next week, when I went back, I was able to get a big laugh simply by paying with a 10, getting my change and looking very serious and saying "Hey I gave you a 20". The shock followed by relief and remembering the moment allowed us to re-ignite that funny moment and laugh again. Now he and I have the sort of friendly relationship where trips to the store are a treat.

There is a lot of judgement that has to be used here. You don't want to be referencing things too often, because it will seem like that is all you do. And you have to be sure that the moment you're referencing has enough significance to that person to jar their memory. So if you're referencing a movie they like, you need to make sure it's one they really like. And if it's a moment, it has to be a big enough moment that they instantly remember it. Basically, the more time that has passed, the bigger the laugh had to have been for the reference to work. So you can call back to a decent laugh that happened an hour ago, but if you're referencing something from a year ago it had better have been a big enough a laugh for that person to remember. You're going to make mistakes with this, but it's worth the struggle because this is a very easy and consistent way to make people laugh and also build friendships by referencing shared past moments.

4.3 That Reminds Me Of...

If you've ever watched a comedy central roast, you're familiar with this concept. A pretty solid percentage of roast jokes are of the format "You look like ________ with ________." For instance, I've got a skinny friend who somehow still has spiked blond hair and bad facial hair and he's a dead ringer for an anorexic Guy Fieri. It's not obvious when you first see him, but once it's pointed out people can't help but laugh. The surprise familiarity causes a spark in our brains that can't be ignored.

Obviously you don't want to walk around tossing roast jokes at everyone, but the concept can be applied in a nicer way to people, and to inanimate objects and animals as well.

If you can train your brain to be able to spot these likenesses, you can moonwalk your way to some easy laughs. And it doesn't have to be celebrities, it can be anyone that both you and the audience are familiar with. I'm using celebrities for context, more people know them than know my Guy Fieri looking friend. But the point is, anytime you can surprise people with a visual familiarity like this you should jump at the chance.

The trick to recognizing these dopplegangers is a little bit counterintuitive. You don't want to try to remember people in detail, you want to reduce everyone to a couple of distinctive features. That way it's much easier to determine what looks like them. For instance, an elephant seal doesn't actually look like Adrian Brody, but it does have a huge nose and spread apart eyes. Those two distinctive features are enough for a recognizable connection. So, if you remember Adrian Brody as a big nose and eyes that are in different time zones, it might not be very nice, but it makes it infinitely easier to determine if something looks like him. Think of them as keywords that help you search through your rolodex of references. Obviously if you're remembering people that you know by distinctive features be careful of offending them.

Although we've only talked about visual referencing so far, the same can be applied to your other senses as well. You can recognize snippets of speech and make references as well. If someone drops a few *alrights* in a row you can compliment them on their Matthew McConaughey. Ditto for smells or tastes that remind you of other things. Again, the trick is to remember things in keywords that other people will recognize, then match up the distinctive features. As with everything, it's going to take practice, but it's yet another way to make people laugh without a ton of legwork to create the joke.

4.4 Hollywood Squares

This horrible show had celebrities of varying stature inside a giant tic-tac-toe board who would get asked questions that they had to answer. The contestant would then have to decide if they thought the celebrity gave the correct answer or not. It's about as boring as it sounds, so to spice it up they decided that every time a celebrity was asked a question, they would first give a little joke answer before they gave their real answer. This is literally the only entertainment value in the show, but it somehow stayed on the air for 40 years. There's definitely a lesson to be learned here.

Every time you get asked a question, it's an opportunity to make a joke. Think about comedians on late night talk shows: the host will ask them a seemingly innocuous question and the comedian will spin it into a funny response or a fully fledged anecdote. You're not going to want to answer every question your answered with a joke, but by taking a look to see if one is there every time you can start consistently using questions as set ups for laughter.

The process is like this:

1. **Analyze the question**: Is this a request for information, or making conversation? Is the request urgent or can I take my time? Is the question open ended or direct? Are they looking for personal information? I want to know the intent of the question so I can determine if it's appropriate to make a joke or if I should just shut up and answer. If someone is asking me what my favourite kind of ice cream is I can probably take the time to try to be funny, whereas if someone is asking me where their EpiPen is I should probably shut up and answer.

2. **Analyse the Environment:** I want to be aware of where I am and who is around me to check if it's ok to make a

joke. If I'm at a bar with friends, of course. If I'm at a funeral, maybe keep it to yourself.

If you run through the first two steps and determine that yes, it's an appropriate time to try to make a joke, move on to step 3. Otherwise abort the process and wait for the next chance.

3. **Guess the Expected Response:** Next, I want to try to determine what I think they think I will say. Most people ask a question with an idea what the answer will be, if I know what they are expecting to hear, then I am way ahead in making a joke out of it. Because as we've learned, the root source of most laughter is surprise. If I know what they're expecting to hear, I can tell them something that is a long way from that and catch them off guard.

4. **A)** If the expected response is short, I usually want my joke response to also be short. A long response to a question that expects a short one is annoying for everyone. What I want to do is come up with a response that is the same length as the expected one, but the opposite of what they were expecting. You want them to have to pause for a second to realize that you're not being serious.

   For example:
    Friend: "What would you like for dinner?"
   Expected Response: "I don't know, pizza?"

5. Now I take that expected response and try to come up with something that is as different as possible.

   Joke Response: "Anything but the flesh of a virgin, I had that for lunch"

You want to craft your response so that it technically answers the question, this causes an extra pause in the audience before they get it. Keeping the joke short avoids annoyance to the listener, especially if it doesn't get a laugh, and allows you to then give a straight answer immediately after.

B) If the expected response is longer, or the question is open ended, then you have a lot more freedom to craft your answer. This can be especially useful for creating interesting and sustained conversation, as a straight answer can often be a dead end. I like to call these situations "**free balls**" which is a volleyball term that refers to a casual bump over the net that the other team is then free to do with what they want. The same is true here, which makes the response less straightforward, but gives you more options with how to proceed.

Think of something as mundane as "What is your favourite movie?" The question is a bit open, because it's asked by a person trying to learn about you. The actual movie isn't the important part, but what it says about you. They want to know not just the movie, but why. This is an opportunity to show something about you, and also make it funny.

Here you must take a step back and realize that because this isn't an inquiry for important information, you don't have to be 100% accurate in your answer. If you say a movie that isn't your absolute favourite, there's no penalty. You don't go to jail or anything. So instead of taking that moment to think about what movie you like the best, think about what movie you liked for a funny reason. Maybe you saw it in theatres super high and you thought the dinosaurs were coming out at you. Maybe you had to watch a sex scene with your parents and the discomfort was hilarious. Maybe you didn't even see the movie because you were busy making out with your first crush. The movie isn't the important thing, the important thing is taking this opportunity to relay a funny story about yourself.

Don't be discouraged if you get asked a question like this and you don't have a good answer. That's perfectly normal. But here's where you can work to change it. When you get asked a question like this that you don't have a funny answer for, remember it. Think about it. Take the next few days and mull it over in your mind and find that funny answer. Step back from the truth, and think about what could've happened instead of what did happen, and what could have been different to make the moment funnier.

Here's an example from my life. For as long as I can remember, I've disliked Steve Carell. For no reason. Just the look of his face makes me angry. I know that I'm wrong and he's very talented and funny, but looking at him fills me with rage. And whenever I say that, people ask me why I don't like him. Here's what I say: Years and years ago when I was young and on the road as a comedian, I met a lady in a town after a show. We had a few drinks and a lovely evening, and at the end of it we went back to my hotel. Things started getting a little physical, but then at one point she stopped me and told me we shouldn't continue, as she had an infection in the fun bits. So instead of having sex, we watched the movie Evan Almighty starring Steve Carrel on the hotel entertainment system, costing me a whopping $19.95. So I sat there aroused and infuriated as this awful movie played out for 96 minutes, and I've hated Steve Carrel ever since.

Now technically speaking, that story isn't true. It's an amalgamation of several different stories and a host of embellishments. But it's an interesting answer that makes people laugh, so it doesn't matter that it isn't accurate. By taking the time to reflect on questions that you're asked, you not only create a library of prepared responses that make you look quick witted and effortlessly interesting, but you work out the muscle that creates those answers allowing you to create swifter responses in the future.

6. **Honestly Evaluate the Reaction:** Take careful note of the response that you get from your answers. If people seem uncomfortable, know that you need to change your approach. If people don't laugh where you think they should, assume that you're wrong and re-evaluate. If you aren't honest with yourself about how people are perceiving you, you'll never improve. In comedy they tell you to never blame the audience, and that goes doubly true in everyday life. Your goal is to entertain this person, if they aren't entertained, it's on you.

Get a Laugh Right Now
Ask the Right Questions

In the next section I'll explain how funny questions are a dead end, which is true when you're trying to get to know someone. But if the interaction is meant to be quick, a funny joke question can break the ice. An example would be an interaction with a cashier or waiter.

Self deprecation works nicely:

What would you recommend for a fat guy looking to get fatter?

You'll have to excuse me I'm incredibly stupid, where are your bananas?

Shared Context is appropriate as you don't know the person:

If it gets any colder can you do me a favour and shoot me in the face?

Listen, you don't want to be here, I don't want to be here, what do you say we take everything out of the till and high tail it to Mexico?

Never make fun of the person or the establishment. Always make fun of yourself or the surroundings. With some practice you'll have a number of great opening questions guaranteed to get a laugh.

4.5 Play Journalist

The other end of the spectrum from answering questions is asking them. This is an excellent chance to show that you're interested in what the other person is saying and show that you're interesting by asking interesting questions. The goal here is a bit different than most of the other techniques because the question to be the funny part. A funny question is a dead end because the joke question can't really be asnwered.

The goal in asking questions is to steer the conversation in a funny direction. You want to ask questions that get the other person thinking in a funny way, so you can then create a funny moment instead of a one-off joke.

First, to encourage conversation, you want your questions to require more than just a yes/no answer. Instead of asking "is that fun?" ask "what is the most fun part of it?" I mean, ideally don't ask either of those, ask something more interesting. But in a structural sense, I hope you see what I mean. Always phrase your question in such a way that it requires the listener to think, and then give a more detailed answer. If you give them an interesting question that allows them to give an interesting answer, there's a good chance there will be room to grow humor from it.

It all sounds easy on paper until you realize – wait, how do I come up with interesting questions. Part of it is going to come down to the work you do on your lateral thinking, but let's try to give you some ideas. I find it's always easiest to learn from examples, so let's try that. First let's start with jobs, because that tends to be the thing adults are most comfortable talking about for whatever reason. Let's say you know that the person you're speaking to is a nurse, you want to think up questions that a nurse wouldn't normally hear. They always hear boring things like *where do you work, what kind of nurse are you, are you a naughty nurse, etc.* You want to think of something that gives them a chance to say something interesting. So you need to put yourself in the shoes of a nurse, and think of what kind of funny situation a nurse might be in. Think of as many as you can (the more you practice the quicker this becomes) and try to form the best one into a question. For example, here are some interesting things about nurses that I would be curious about:

- Is patient body odour as huge a factor as I'd expect?

- Have you ever had a patient who was obviously faking for drugs?

- Are there as many affairs in hospitals as it seems on TV?

If this is a person that you're trying to impress, you can tailor the questions to be more complimentary to the job. Like:

- Nurses are the saintliest people because they do most of the work and get none of the credit, why do you think nurses are so overlooked?

- You guys have to do all of the dirty work for everyone, do people appreciate what you do enough?

The key is to lock in on something that is agreeable and interesting to the person you're speaking with. By asking questions that you are actually interested in you'll be more engaged in the answers, and this helps create **shared context**. You have to then listen intently to the answer so that you can continue to search for ways to get laughs.

So, in the case of the body odor question, I know that regardless of the nurse's answers, I should be able to find some humor. I assume they will say yes, because my belief is that a lot of people stink. If I'm right, then I can gently prod them for examples that I know will be funny, because the question I've asked lends itself to humorous answers. If they say no, then I can feign surprise and ask more leading questions.

By asking leading questions and digging for interesting information you can not only keep the conversation interesting, you can create opportunities for jokes. It's more than just being funny, it's being the kind of funny that draws people to you.

4.6 A New Angle

When in a group conversation, a lot of the time is spent discussing issues on topics, usually current events. Small talk is always that or the weather, and for the most part, it's unbearably bland. A good way to appear more interesting is to learn how to form unique opinions about commonly discussed topics. You want to make sure that the opinion you have, whether you actually believe it or not, is different than what everyone else is saying. As with everything, there are levels to it.

At the most basic level is a sarcastic response. If you're in a group discussing a topic that everyone agrees on you can get a laugh by simply stating that you believe the opposite. At the time of writing, it is 2020 and Trump is in charge, so 65% of the conversations I hear are about his rampant idiocy. So, if I'm with a group and they've been bashing The Donald for 2 minutes and everyone is in complete agreement, I can get a laugh just by saying "I don't know guys, I think he's doing a pretty good job." It causes that moment of shock, followed by the relief of recognition that I'm not serious.

4.7 Sarcasm

Sarcasm is a bit complicated because there's a real subtlety to it – not just to make it funny, but also to make it pleasant for the audience. The essence of sarcasm is to completely belittle something, so sometimes sarcasm can become grating on the listener. It's sort of like constant negativity, it drags people down. The way to avoid that is to avoid being sarcastic about anything the audience cares deeply about. If they love Third Eye Blind and they get excited when it comes on, only to have you sarcastically say *oh yeah this is music at its absolute peak*, it takes the wind out of their sails. You want to try to only be sarcastic when you know you're on the same side as the audience.

For example, if you're on a plane waiting to take off and the pilot comes over the intercom and says *we're going to be delayed another 20 minutes as we wait for a runway*, you could turn to your seatmate with mock excitement and say *that's exactly what I wanted him to say! I love the runway.* This way you know that the audience agrees and will respond well to your sarcasm.

When you're being sarcastic, you want to do your absolute darndest to make sure that the audience knows you're being sarcastic. It's super uncomfortable when you say something sarcastically and the listener believes you. Now they'll live the rest of their lives thinking you actually do love Big Bang Theory. You want to make sure you have a sarcastic tone, but more importantly you want to use a little bit of hyperbole to accentuate. If *Who Let the Dogs Out?* starts blaring on the radio and you say *I like this song!*, it's not clear you're being sarcastic. If you instead say *I don't know who I'm going to marry but I know this song will be our first dance* it's a little more obvious that you're being sarcastic. If you find people aren't getting your sarcasm, consider upping the exaggeration.

4.8 Self Deprecation

I'll talk more about specific uses of self deprecation later on, but the idea is that making yourself the victim of the joke puts everyone else at ease. No one is worried if the victim is upset because that's you. It also shows that you don't take yourself too seriously, which relaxes the audience further. You can make fun of yourself in a number of different ways depending on how familiar they are with you. You want to keep in mind context before you delve into making fun of yourself, because as I've mentioned, the audience might not perceive you the same way that you perceive yourself. You want to make fun of the things that other people will agree with.

Only make fun of things about yourself that you would be comfortable having other people make fun of as well. If it's something that actually bothers you, don't joke about. First, people can tell when you're actually sad. If you're trying to joke to cover up some actual sadness you're dealing with, it's going to come across as less of a joke and more of a sad fact. You want to joke about insignificant things. And second, if you make fun of yourself enough about something, eventually other people will make the same jokes. If you don't want that to happen, don't joke about it yourself.

Making fun of yourself paints you in a modest and humble light which draws people towards you. But again – only if they think you're funny and not sad. Your self-deprecation cannot be too harsh, and it can't make other people pity you. If there is no confidence behind it, do not use it. It has to be something that you actually find funny about yourself.

Self deprecation proves that you are an equal opportunity attacker. Meaning you'll have a lot more leeway making fun of others if you also throw some shots at yourself sometime. Make sure to always gauge the audience's reaction to make sure they're not being bummed out by your negativity though, it's easy to become a pity case if you're constantly putting yourself down.

This should give you a solid base for how to be funny in the moment, but I can't stress enough that it only works if you practice it. Try things out and see what works for you.

Chapter 5 – Proactively Funny

Being proactively funny, by my definition, is having set pieces pre-prepared that you can use at any time without any sort of set up. That's an annoyingly vague definition, because to me it covers a wide range of things. Everything from storytelling to writing emails to icebreaker lines to initiating text messages. The defining factor to me is that you have time to prepare what you're going to say, and you're going to need to provide both the set up and the punch line for it to work. With reactively funny the set up is something external, and you are creating a joke from that. Pro-active is all you baby. You've got to build it from the ground up.

The dirty secret behind funny people is that they take a lot of time to practice and prepare. They repeat themselves a lot when they find something that works, and they know how to make it sound organic.

The more work you put into it, the better your results will be. When you have the time to prepare something that you want to be funny, take the time to really do it. Especially if you're not "naturally" funny, preparation can really help overcome your inexperience. In fact, if you're having a hard time developing the reactively funny skills I described earlier, focusing on proactive techniques can be a great idea. If people don't think you're funny in the moment, you can surprise them with your proactive skills and make them realize there is more to you than they think. Because you have the time to prepare, you can outwork everyone to be funny – even if it doesn't flow out of you in the moment.

I'm going to show you some examples, but the main idea that you need to always keep in mind is that you can find places to insert humor in things that you need to prepare. A cover letter, an email to a friend, a presentation: they can all be an opportunity to be funny. When you have the time to prepare, you can find a way to be appropriately funny, you just have to look. We'll go over specific examples of appropriate for specific situations later in the book, but for now let's look at some broader ideas.

5.1 Storytelling

Far and away the greatest skill you can have to be proactively funny is storytelling. And I when I say storytelling, I don't mean like an old man spouting off with some *once upon a time* marathon tale.

I mean the ability to relay an event to a person or group in a funny and interesting way. I can't teach you how to tell a riveting and compelling story that tugs at the heartstrings and teaches wise lessons, I'm not an old sensei or something. What I want to try to do is show you how to extract the funny out of your experience and distil it down to the point that it is consistently funny.

Let's start with a few general tips for telling funny stories:

Shorter is better: When you're trying to make something funny, you want to trim away as much of the unnecessary information as possible. Ideally, anything that isn't vital to the plot or vital to the humor should be gone. Don't add extra details that don't serve any purpose. If you're telling a story about a shirt, and you go out of your way to mention that the shirt is purple, the color purple better play into the story down the line. Otherwise, the listener is left wonder "Why the hell do I need to know that it's purple?" You want to keep people's focus on the important details and not muddy the water with all this other garbage.

There's no easy rule of thumb for how long your story should be, but you want each part to either be driving the story forward or be working on a laugh. Anything else is just fat on the meat of your story. And while a little bit of fat *can* be ok, you want to make a habit of cutting it off.

Finish Strong

You want the very end of your story to be the funniest part, so try to keep the tension built until the end. The last funny reveal plus the satisfaction from a good conclusion makes a solid period at the end of the story. If the story makes it impossible to keep the funniest bit until the end, you still need to find a way to wrap it up on a laugh. You want to make it clear that this story is over.

Add funny intervals

You want the biggest laugh of your story to be at the end, but you don't want people to get bored in the middle. You need to be honest with yourself and look at parts of the story that are the least interesting and try to bolster those with some added jokes. Every minute or so of your story you need to have something funny, otherwise people get bored. Try to put yourself in the head of the listener and identify what parts need some love and sit down and work on them.

Be Your Own Worst Critic

When you're adding humor to your story, be hypercritical about your choices. If you're adding something purely for the sake of getting a laugh it had better get one, because if not, you start to

lose the confidence of your audience. People will let you take liberties if they know it's going to pay off at the end, but if you start swinging and missing, people will start to tune out.
If you're trying spice up a vital piece of information the threshold isn't nearly as strong because the plot is moving along. Feel free to take more chances when conveying information because people will have more patience. But when you're doing it purely for the laughs, you had better connect.

Train your Brain
Critique yourself like a pro

It's incredibly difficult to honestly evaluate your own stories. You're too close to it to have an unbiased view into the funny level of story. It makes being your own critic much harder than it appears. Here's a little trick to help.

Write your story down.

Word for word. Write it all out. The act of writing out the words gives you a new perspective on what you're saying. You'll have a better appreciation for the structure of your story.

Edit your story

I guarantee the first draft can be improved. Try to read the story through the eyes of someone with no context. Make sure you've told them what they need to know, and no more. Remove extra information and re-arrange parts to make more sense and be funnier. Any time you go a long time without something funny, add something funny in.

Never go more than a paragraph or two without a laugh.

Either add laughs or remove filler until you've got a tight, punchy, ready-to-tell story. Writing it down allows better editing and imprints the story on your brain so you'll tell it better next time. Professional comedians do it for a reason.

Based on a True Story

Don't get too weighed down in relaying *exactly* what happened. You're telling a story, not reporting the news. Your main goal is to entertain the listener, so facts are secondary. You're allowed to exaggerate, change dates and figures, and alter details to make the story more interesting. Think to yourself, what small changes could have happened to have made it funnier? Maybe a horse kicked you in the thigh when you were 5, but it's a way better story if he kicked you in the face. Don't be afraid to rewrite history.

If you get too firmly attached to the facts, your story becomes dry and underwhelming. Everyone's life is boring, but if you learn to embellish and liven up a story you can turn your *huh, neat* story into a *wow, really?* The real skill of the process is being able to assess your situation and know how far from the truth you can deviate. It depends on the story, the audience, and the environment, but you should watch out for a couple of things.

- Is there anyone present who was there for the event who might contradict your story? If so, you want to steer closer to the truth.
- Is there anyone present who is a known contrarian destined to question your lies? This can be frustrating but can also be an opportunity to turn it around on that contrarian. If the story has gone over well, you have the momentum, so a quick response can really win the rest of the crowd over. You'll need to develop your own style for how to deal with whatever version of "That never happened!" but a quick one liner can cut them down. Or alternatively, if attacking people isn't your style, you either own up to changing some details or give a vague non-committal response. Here are some examples:

Aggressive:

What are you, the story police? Let me see your badge

Admissive:

Some details have been changed to help move the

story along, you're welcome

Vague:

Truth is all about perception, I just speak my truth

Be Fluid

If you watch a lot of stand-up comedy one thing you'll notice is that bits and routines evolve over time. It does more than just improve the story too; it keeps it fresh in your mind. One of the dangers of telling the same story repeatedly is that you will eventually start to go into autopilot. You'll be telling the story without thinking about it, and after you do that long enough all the passion is gone. You tell it dead behind the eyes, and the story loses its impact. By constantly changing and tinkering with your stories, you can keep them fresh and fun for both you and the audience.

You're not under investigation by the FBI, your story doesn't have to be exactly the same every time. Try different things, and don't be afraid to drop what isn't working. Allow your mind to wander and exaggerate and let the story grow on its own. Getting caught up in a rigid story is like getting caught up in the truth, it leads you down a path to boredom. Allow your story to be a living thing, let it grow and evolve. And honestly, let it die too. People get sick of hearing the same thing over and over again, so when your story gets too old to entertain, do the right thing and put it out to pasture.

Pay Attention to Your Audience

Let's just say it straight: sometimes you bore people. We all do. It doesn't matter how funny you are, some people just aren't going to like you. If you're in the middle of a story and you are completely losing the attention of the other party, there's no shame in ducking out early. Don't take it personally, but don't force it. If you are continually forcing people to listen to stories that they don't want to hear, you're going to find yourself alone a lot.

Watch people's eyes, if they aren't focused on you, you're losing them. It's not always your fault, but it's up to you to pull the chute and get out. Make sure your stories have an escape valve that you can use in case of emergencies. Boring is the opposite of funny, so err on the side of caution and shut the hell up.

Be Animated

Just like pictures help draw you into a book, physical gesturing can help draw you into a story. When you're telling your story, try to think of ways that you can add an element of physicality to it. I don't mean act it out like it's a Shakespearean play or something, but subtle physical gestures help explain things that words can't. One of the prime rules of filmmaking is "show, don't tell", and you can apply that idiom to your storytelling. Any detail that you can show as opposed to explain will help in a couple of ways.

First of all, from a pure structural standpoint, act outs save you words. Remember, we want to cut out all the fat, so by showing how someone was standing as opposed to explaining it, you're cutting out a ton. You can explain a lot with gestures, and it will help speed along the boring parts of your story. That alone will improve your communication, but physicality can also add umph to your details.

When you're describing a person, try to act them out. Instead of "the walked towards me", say "they walked towards me like this", and do an exaggerated act out of how they walked. It allows you to get a laugh from imitating them, and also draws people into the story because now they can picture it. This is a great way to add details without sacrificing entertainment. The fat is anything that doesn't move the plot or build to a laugh, so by turning details into jokes you can add more and more layers to your story.

Live in the Moment

The most engaging storytellers are the ones who make you feel like you are actually there, and that is a difficult skill to emulate. Far too many people think that since a picture is worth a thousand words, you need a thousand words to paint someone a picture. It might seem a bit counterintuitive, but one of the best ways to make people *feel like they are there* is to make *yourself* feel that way. When you tell the story, try to actively remember being there. Not so that you can explain every detail to the person, but so that you can recapture the energy you felt at that moment.

It's that energy that draws people in, not the description itself. The more you can connect to those emotions, the more you convey them. And the emotion is what makes people feel they are there. If you're telling your story and in your head, you are there, you get an energy about you as if you were there, and that draws people in. It sounds a bit like crystals or something, but by being there in your head, your brain recalls the emotions, and it adds to your story. I promise you this is the most hippy thing I'll try to sell you on, but it works.

Hold a Little Back

Don't be afraid to keep some details to yourself, specifically ones you think people will be curious about. Prepare that part of the story, but don't tell it. This way, when someone does ask you, you have a readymade answer that will make you look even better because it will seem as though you came up with it on the spot.

5.2 Creating Stories

For the purposes of this book, we're going to define a "story" as a retelling of a singular event, which is perhaps slightly unconventional. If you went to the mall and you saw a mall Santa punch a father, then you fell in some spaghetti in the food court, then accidentally smashed a $10,000 TV, all before the bus crashed on the way home, you might be tempted to think of the whole thing as the story of your trip to the mall. For trying to make things funny, we're going to break them down another step. We're going to consider each incident its own story, and the trip to the mall is just the folder in our brain we store those in.

This may seem dumb, but it helps us out in a few ways. If we think of the trip to the mall as the story, then right out the gate we have ourselves trapped in a much longer story. We have to both remember that story and regurgitate it, both of which can sometimes be tedious. By breaking it down into smaller chunks it becomes easier to remember and shorter to tell, both good benefits. Also, by making the scope of each story smaller we give ourselves the chance to add a bit more detail to each story and really milk the laughs for all they're worth. With a longer, multi-tier story people tend to rush to get to the next part and don't get full value out of each story.

The other hidden benefit of breaking the stories down into manageable chunks is now you'll remember each one individually. So instead of remembering "I have a good story about the mall", you know you have four good stories about four different topics. This is crucial in conversation, because typically the way our brains work is that a topic will come up and it will trigger our memory of a story. So if you remember it as *my mall story*, then when people are talking about the mall, you'll go "oh, I have a good mall story" and you can let it fly. But by having four different topics, you're much more likely to hit a point where you get the chance to tell one of them. And by having a funny story for every topic, you become someone who is consistently funny.

Events

If a story is a retelling of a single event, what constitutes an event? It can be anything really – anything that you experience in any way that you think will be interesting to others. Obviously, some events are inherently more interesting than other; getting hit by a car is more interesting than blowing your nose. It's more difficult than it sounds because everyone has a different threshold of interesting. To 99.9% of the world, getting your black belt in Tai Kwan Do would be an interesting event for a story, but at The World Tai Kwan Doe Black Belt Conference it's boring. As always, **context** is important to keep in mind.

Regardless of the event, you can make it interesting. The rub is, the less inherently impressive the event is, the more you have to work to make it interesting. At the World Tai Kwan Doe Black Belt Conference, a story about getting your black belt isn't inherently interesting, but if you got your black belt on the moon, it's suddenly got people's attention.

Theoretically you can make just about anything funny and interesting if you work hard enough, but the more interesting the event, the easier it will be.

You want the event to be as precise a moment as possible, so that you can't use it to anchor the story. That moment is going to be the thing you build up to the entire time, and from that moment we can work backwards to build our story. This moment is the whole reason that you're telling the story. There can be lots of other interesting and funny moments in the story, but this is the crux. If the story is about you getting hit by a car, that moment is when you get hit. The rest of the story is what led up to that moment. There may be more to the story after, but that is the centerpiece of the whole ordeal.

An added bonus of picking a single interesting event is that you have a built-in tease to get people interested in the story. In fact, if you're confident in your story, you can tell them the end as a tease and draw them in for the entire story. Movies do it all the time, show you the end and then flashback and go through the movie. It's a great way to keep interest and build suspense throughout your story. And you can use it to sell your story; a title if you will. All these little things help you get ahead.

Story Construction

Once you have your event, your next job is to start putting together the story. Keep in mind, our "story" could be two sentences about you falling over at the grocery store, but by doing this homework for everything you plan to tell people, you can ensure whatever you relay is going to be both funny and interesting.

Before you can figure out how to tell the story, you need to determine how much **context** you need to build. What information does the listener need to know to appreciate the event? What background information do I need to provide for the event to trigger the emotional response I'm expecting? You have to look at the event objectively and decide what information is pertinent, and what isn't.
After you've made a list of all of the necessary information, you want to then take stock of the funny or interesting things that happened leading up to the event. Try to be hypercritical when selecting these as they are unnecessary to the story. So if and when you pick something that turns out to be less funny than you think, you've added fat to your story. And as I mentioned above, you lose the confidence of your audience.

Now that you have all the necessary information and all of the spicy bits picked out, you have all the ingredients for your story. All we have to do now is make the cake. You have to find a way to mash all of these bits together and come out with a fluid story. This is the part where you want to start letting go of that firm grasp of the truth, and start massaging things to fit together. Take what happened and let it melt together with what happened in your head. Let time flow like sand so that your story all happens at the same time instead of over the course of several days.

Obviously, this is going to take practice. For starters, you can simply straight up tell them all of the parts separately like some sort of robot. *Here is some background information, here is something funny that happened. Here is some more background, now here is the event.* Say it out loud to yourself and you'll notice that it doesn't flow. Let go of the absolute truth and change small details to make it flow better. Keep saying it out loud, your brain will help you start to mold it into a cohesive structure. This is how stories take shape. If you stick to just the important and funny bits, you can speak it into existence. You just have to listen and be honest with yourself and make changes.

Example

Let me walk you through an example. This is a story that I tell sometimes to the point that it's a struggle to remember the truth. The story is about the time I kind of met William Shatner (tease). So let me break down the story using the methods I've shown above:

Event: Met William Shatner

Background Information: William Shatner is a famous celebrity, we were both working at a comedy festival so we were at the same party, I don't particularly like William Shatner's work, I'm a righteous coward

For complete transparency, I'll write the story as *it actually happened* using the facts presented above, and then I'll write the story *as I tell it*. You'll notice there's a drastic difference and I'm a liar, but I'm here to entertain and the truth is open to interpretation.

Actual:
Title – When I Almost Met Shatner

When I was very new to comedy, I was invited to the Just For Laugh's Festival in Montreal. Also performing that year (not on any show I was on) was William Shatner, who you may know as Captain Kirk from Star Trek. Or if you're under 25 you probably don't know at all. Regardless, was and is very famous. All of the acts stay at the same hotel, so if you sit in the bar you can see everyone. I'm there, sitting by myself like a loser because my friend had to leave after he laughed too hard and got a bit of pee in his pants. All of the sudden I hear a commotion, and in walks Shatner and his wife, and a mob of people run towards him. I think to myself "I could meet William Shatner", but there are lots of people there already and I barely know who he is so I don't bother. Eventually he leaves and I keep being lonely. End of story.

It's not super interesting, but it's enough that you could tell people and have them go "huh, neat". But by realizing its weaknesses and making slow, steady improvements, I now tell it like this:

Reworked:

Title - I snubbed William Shatner once.

I was at the comics bar backstage at a show at Just For Laugh's in 2011 having a drink with a few comedians when we hear a bit of a commotion, and in walks William Shatner. He had been hosting a show around the corner and popped over. Everyone in the bar loses their minds and stands up to rush to meet him, including my friend, who was hammed and got a little too excited and pissed pants. My buddy took his piss puddle and left, so it's just me watching Shatner. And he was shaking hands and saying hello to everybody. And before I even knew what I was doing, I was in line to meet him too. Cause it's Captain Kirk right? Who doesn't want to meet Captain Krik?

But as I'm getting close to him, I realize... I hate Star Trek. I hate his singing. In fact, I don't like anything he's ever done. I'm only meeting him because he's famous. What has this society done to me to make me drool over this man purely because of celebrity? Look, I was 23, I got all self righteous, and just as he was about to shake my hand I pulled it away and walked right past him like a cocky little asshole. I thought I was really sticking it to him but I looked back and I don't think he even noticed. Worst part is now I really wish I had met him.

Let's look at what I've done. First of all, I've changed myself to be far more active in the story than the original. It makes it feel more personal. I've changed the setting to be more intimate and impressive, and made myself sound less alone because I'm vain. The entire interaction with him happened in my head, but I've worked it into the story because it adds tension and interest. Notice that the overall theme, as well as the ending, are essentially the same. I don't actually cause a change to what occurred, but it adds a lot more spice. I use a lot of self deprecation to make sure the listeners don't think that I think I'm being a cool guy for doing this. I want them to know that I'm the person to laugh at here, and I'm ok with it. By changing it and making me the fool I'm not being insulting to anyone in the story but myself, which allows me to be an ass but still be likeable, since I've learned my lesson. And I've also prepared myself for follow up questions. For instance, one obvious one would be "Did he say anything?" to which I say "nah I'm sure it happens all the time, I'm not the only asshole out there." Again, further distancing myself from the actions and keeping my likability intact. Also, by giving an answer that adds no interest I discourage further follow up questions.

The story is short, but I still try to add a couple of laughs in the middle. I change the timing of the pants pissing for dramatic effect, and the realization that I hate Star Trek gets a laugh because I've built up my excitement for Captain Kirk. It's not that much of a drastic change, but it does drastically change how the story is perceived, as well as how people perceive me after hearing it. These are all things you need to think about when telling a story.

Mull it over
Tell a great story every time

The greatest stories are ones that are told over and over again. There's a reason for this – as they're repeatedly told, they transform and tighten to the point that only the interesting and funny information is left. To become a good storyteller, you need to learn to do this yourself with your stories. No matter how small the story is, you need to say it aloud (or in your head) over and over again until it feels right. Modify and edit until the story is compelling the entire time.

Ask yourself the following questions:

- Does my story end at the climax? Always end with the best part
- Does my story have a compelling start? If there isn't a great start, create one. Find or invent tension to act as a hook – the listener needs a nugget to keep them interested.
- Does my story have unnecessary details? If a detail doesn't entertain or add to the plot, drop it.
- Does my story have intermediary punchlines? To keep the reader engaged you need to add jokes in the middle of your story. You can do this by adding details, explaining your thoughts, or simply making something up. If you're telling the story to yourself and there is a minute with nothing funny or amazing – **add it!**
- Is my story too long? If it feels like it drags to you, it definitely will to them. **Edit, edit, edit.**

5.3 Other Ways to be Proactive

While storytelling is likely to be the most important skill you can develop, the real secret to proactive comedy is to always be searching for places you can insert humor. Anytime you need to write, speak, or present is a chance for you to add a splash of funny. Here are some specific examples.

Email

Nobody likes reading or writing emails – it's all the bad parts of a letter with none of the good. But if you look at them as an opportunity to be funny, they become a little less monotonous. Email is a tricky medium to be really funny though, so you want to downplay things a bit. You want to be sure not to add too many unnecessary words, as reading them is already a chore. Try to keep your jokes short, non-ambiguous, and on topic for the email. Don't deviate from the subject for the sake of a joke unless it's a single line. Anything else and people will start to hate getting emails from you.

You also have to be careful with what kind of jokes you use, because a lot of things that could be funny if you spoke to them won't be funny in print. People underestimate how much they add to a joke when they talk. Their tone, body language and facial expressions help to convey when something is supposed to be funny, and all of that is lost in text. As such, the best tactic for funny emails is usually cleverness – wordplay and self deprecation can work well. If you're talking about a shared issue you can poke fun at the issue. Try to avoid sarcasm or insult directed at people, neither read properly through text.

A good rule of thumb when trying to write something funny is to write it, save it, and then come back and read it several hours later. Email gives us this luxury, and you'd be wise to use it. I can't tell you how many times I've written something that I thought was hilarious at the time, only to come back later and wonder what the hell I was thinking. Re-reading your email later with fresh eyes will give you much more subjective opinion of your writing.

Keep in mind that jokes that bomb in an email are super annoying to the reader. It wastes their time and energy, and it makes them think less of you. Plus, it's a black and white receipt of you not being funny that they can always look back on. My point is that if you're unsure if what you're writing is funny or not, don't write it. You always need to take chances, but emails aren't the best place to do it.

Text/Instant Messaging

The more conversational nature of messaging lends itself to jokes a lot more than stuffy old email, but you still have to be very careful of tone. The person on the other end has to read it, and quite often any semblance of sarcasm or irony will be completely lost. You need to take time with your wording to ensure that you are getting across the point that you mean to be getting across, and that nothing will get lost. Again, don't rush your response, take time to read and re-read to make sure you're being clear.

The informal nature of texts also means that you can open a conversation with a joke, which is one of the more powerful forms of proactive humor. These opening jokes are a blank canvas that you can use to create jokes. You have nothing to work off, which can be scary, but it also means that everything is on the table. Essentially, in the same way that Tweets can be funny, openings to conversations can be as well.

In the second half of the book, we'll go through some more specific examples, but the idea is that you want something that is unexpected, but not random, if that makes sense. You want it to be something that merits a response. Attempting to be random for the sake of random is a conversational ender, not a starter. For example, here would be a way to randomly open a message:

People who wear yellow hats are really mice in

disguise.

It's unexpected and succinct, but what in the hell is someone going to say back to that? The most hilarious randomness in the world gets at best a "LOL what?" in return. Instead you want to say something unexpected that invites questions. You don't want this joke to be the end, you want it to be the start. Even if random thoughts are your thing, if you changed the above to:

> *I saw a guy in a yellow hat today, I'm pretty sure he was a mouse in disguise.*

Now assuming you know this person well enough to say this garbage to them, they may have some questions. By personalizing it and making it an experience or opinion that you have, you're opening the door for further conversation. This isn't the line I'd use, but the principal is such that you want the unexpected thing to seem interesting about you. You want to have the quirky experiences and thoughts, and you want to share those in such a way that they invite follow up questions.

Opening lines aside, being continuously funny throughout a messaging conversation sort of blurs the line between reactive and proactive comedy, since you are being responsive, but you have time to plan your responses. And you should do that. Before you respond with a funny message, take the time to really think over the conversation. Pay special attention to the context and workshop your ideas before you respond. Almost never will your first gut response be the funniest thing you can think of, so don't stop there. Try to find a better joke. If you do this every time, then you will keep ending up with better and better jokes.

We'll go over messaging in more specific and practical detail in the second part of this book.

Speeches/Presentations

Most people are terrified of public speaking, but if you're confident in your humor, a speech becomes a great opportunity to show off. The first speech I ever gave was in high school when I ran for student council president. I didn't care about politics, but I thought I could write a funny speech. I wrote it all out and was excited, but was absolutely terrified of public speaking. I had never done it, and I certainly didn't think I could do it. But after I read my first joke in a stammering voice and it got a big laugh, my whole body eased. Hearing the whole room laugh lets you know that they are listening, and they value what you have to say.

As such, you should treat any public speaking engagement (short of eulogies or public apologies) as a chance to make people laugh. Not just for them, but for you too. It will bolster your confidence and make your speech a memorable one. Most people aren't funny, if you can be, you'll stand out.

To make a speech funny, you want to add to it without taking away from your message. The best way to do that is to write your speech out in a dry, unfunny way first. You want to be sure that you say everything you need to say. After that, you can go back through it and do what the entertainment industry calls *punch up*. That is, take something that isn't funny, and make it funny. By creating the skeleton of the speech first, you can add in jokes without detracting from the message. You'll want to read it back to yourself out loud and try to find places where you can add jokes. You'll likely have to massage the existing words to make it work, but that's ok.

The sort of jokes that work the best in speeches are jokes about the people present, the place you're currently in, the subject at hand, and yourself. Anytime you can include an audience member (that the others are familiar with) in a joke, you will get a crazy response from the audience, I promise you. Whether you're at a wedding or a board meeting, jokes about those present are always winners. Don't be overly harsh, but feel free to take light shots at those present, as long as you also take shots at yourself. You need to show that you're not above it.

You should also start the speech with a joke, but this can be a bit lengthier and only tangentially related to the topic. It can be a story about yourself and your relation to the occasion, it can be a joke about your qualifications to give the speech, or it can be about the event/location you are in. But try to start with as strong a joke as possible, even at the expense of it being unrelated. By getting a laugh as soon as you start, you're training the audience to see you as a funny person. It sounds odd, but that trust is a huge thing. If you start your speech dry and serious, that's how people perceive you. But sliding in an unexpected joke in the first few sentences tells them that they can't relax, else they might miss something. It keeps the audience engaged and ensures that you are giving yourself the best possible chance to get laughs. Also, getting that first laugh will relax you and give you the confidence to fly through the rest of your presentation.

These are just some of the ways that you can be proactively funny, but they illustrate the main overarching idea – identifying moments where you have the time to make something funny. By understanding where and when you can insert humor, you can stop and brainstorm just the right way to do it. By putting yourself in the headspace where you are hunting for proactively funny moments, you'll train yourself to be keenly aware of these moments. And by understanding that you have the time to get it right you can be sure to maximize your proactive funny.

Get a laugh right now
An early joke sets the tone

If you're like most people, you're uncomfortable speaking in front of people. It's completely normal. Unfortunately, the more nervous you appear, the less comfortable it is for the audience to watch. It's uncomfortable to watch someone uncomfortable. Weirdly, a part of that is the subconscious thought of **do they know how awkward this is?**

Here's a practical tip to instantly put your audience at ease regardless of how uncomfortable you look: **Address your discomfort**.

In stand up we call it *being in the room*. It lets the audience know that you're feeling the same things they are.

If you know you're going to seem uncomfortable, make a joke about it right away. Try something like this:

You'll have to be patient with me, I'm not the best public speaker. I apologize in advance for how difficult it will be for you to find ways to compliment me afterwards.

I'm sorry, I'm a little uncomfortable. They told me to picture all of you in your underwear, but they didn't warn me how ugly you all look naked.

*Before I start, I just want to say I know I'm not the most natural public speaker. I can be a little akward sometimes. Just remember, if you're ever feeling uncomfortable, just know it's **way** worse for me.*

I won't keep you long – trust me, no one wants this to be over more than I do.

Hopefully this goes well, but if not... hey, at least no one will make me speak again.

I'm very excited to be here to speak to you today. I don't get to speak in front of people very often, and soon you'll find out why!

They say that most people's biggest fear is speaking in public, though I've found listening to me speak in public is a close second.

Chapter 6 – Wit

Wit has got to be one of the more difficult things to both define and practice, but it's probably the shortest route to having people think you're smart. I talked a lot about the concepts of cleverness earlier, and being a witty person is someone who combines those concepts with humor to produce smart, insightful comments at a moment's notice. I gave you a lot of concrete methods for searching for funny moments earlier, but wit is a little more generic. It's like strength, you can't teach it, and you have to work at it. In this section I will explain my approach to wit and break down some classic examples so that you can see how others handle it.

The reason we equate wit with intelligence is because being witty involves being well informed on a large enough variety of topics. We mentioned knowledge breadth earlier, and this is where it applies. It's very difficult to joke about a topic without knowing the subtleties, so unfortunately the first step in vamping up your wit is to be well informed. Read, watch, and consume as much as you can. Don't try to be an expert on everything, but try to get an understanding of it to the point that you feel comfortable talking about it. Things that are mentioned a lot (current events, pop culture, sports) are especially important to know, as that is what people are talking about. The more informed you are, the easier it is to be witty.

Beyond just being informed, consuming as much media as you can gives you exposure to all sorts of different types of wit that you can analyze and emulate. Most funny movies and shows are filled with wit, and you can learn a lot from watching them. Keep in mind though that these things are scripted – you'll very rarely be set up as perfectly as they are in real life, and certainly not nearly as consistently.

Although wit can be hard to define, it's usually easy to recognize. So when you're trying to be witty, you need to pause to do some quality assurance before you speak. Again, this is something that takes practice, and at the start, you're going to be slow. Wit has a lot to do with timing, and this can cause problems. By the time you think of something witty and then do a "quality check" to make sure that it is in fact worth saying, the moment may already be gone. It's fine to take chances, but the more you miss, the less confidence people have in you. It's better to say two great jokes and be quiet for the rest of the night, then to have three great ones and seven stinkers.

You can look witty using any of the methods we've gone through, but the general concept of "wit" is to be able to use the appropriate method at the appropriate time. It's essentially your overall ability to be reactively funny. I mentioned earlier the mindset of funny, and this is the ultimate realization of that. Your end goal is to see whatever is happening in front of you as set ups instead of conversations. Everyone is helping you make jokes, you just have to realize it.
As with all humor, we can break down wit into Reactive and Proactive examples.

Reactive

Reactive wit is responding to an outside stimulus quickly with a clever response. With reactive wit timing is at least as important as content, and as with everything this takes practice. Reactive wit involves very quickly assessing the context and crafting a suitable response. It's not easy, but it amazes people. If you're consistently reactively witty people will not only think you're funny, but also much smarter than you are.

Let's break down some classic examples of reactive wit and see what we can learn.

> *Winston Churchill was once at a party, apparently quite drunk, when he had an encounter with a high-class socialite from another political party. The woman turned her nose up at Churchill and said with disdain, "You, sir, are drunk." Churchill, not missing a beat, responded in a dry tone of voice, "You, madam,*

are ugly, and in the morning I shall be sober."

Maybe it's not the most politically correct of moments, but gosh darnit, that lady swung first. Churchill may not have been the greatest leader of all time but he was a great drunk and a great motivator, and this is a fantastic showing.

Obviously, I don't know what was going on in Churchill's mind, but this is what I would imagine the process was:

Chuchill recognized that he was being insulted, but he also recognized that the woman wasn't wrong. Everyone could see that he was drunk, so denial was completely out of the question. Remember that wit is linked to intelligence, and trying to pretend he wasn't drunk would be stupid. He'd look like an even bigger fool. So, knowing that he is in the wrong, the only is thing to do is to lean into what she said (self deprecation) and fire back with an insult.

By admitting that he was drunk, he gains credibility with the crowd, which gives a bigger punch when he fires back. He hones in on something everyone can see (her appearance) and points it out in a beautiful way. Note his wording – he leaves the word ugly until the very end. He hides the punch, building the suspense and cutting the tension on the last word which illicit laughter.

It's really a very simple insult, but the beautiful wording and timing makes it into a classic. This is one of the tricks of wit: the actual subject matter doesn't have to be that clever, you can mask it with timing and wording. Churchill knew that to be appreciated by the mass audience that was present, he needed to reach for something that everyone could appreciate. With a smaller audience that had more intimate knowledge of the woman, he could have perhaps hit on something more specific. But by analyzing his audience and his environment, he was able to show off his wit cleanly and confidently.

Another example:

> *Norm MacDonald was on Conan O'Brien with actor Courtney Thorne-Smith, who was promoting a movie she was in with Carrot Top. MacDonald had been taking shots at Carrot Top all night ("I know what a good name for it would be, Box Office Poison") when Thorne-Smith revealed the name of the movie, the fairly innocuous "Chairman of the Board". O'Brien challenged MacDonald "Do something with that, you freak". MacDonald paused, then gushed "I bet board is spelled B-O-R-E-D".*

Perhaps my favourite modern example of wit is Norm MacDonald on late night television with this absolute gem. The entire interview is a showcase of MacDonald's sharpness, it's worth a watch, but this retort at the end was over the top. Before we break it down, let's first take a moment to appreciate how difficult it is to be this witty on demand in front of millions of viewers. That's insane.

In this case he had very little to work with – in terms of context people weren't especially familiar with Carrot Top, but MacDonald had made it very clear that he wasn't a fan. Even Conan had insinuated Carrot Top wasn't especially talented, so that was in the audience's mind. Beyond that, he had only the title. Since very little had been revealed about the movie itself, he couldn't make fun of the content, he had to make a joke out of the title that didn't refer to specific content. In fact, the only thing he could tie it to was the fact that it had been established Carrot Top kind of sucks. So, with those limitations in place, one of the quickest and cleverest solutions is to look at the words themselves.

So instantly MacDonald knew he'd make a joke about how bad the movie/Carrot Top is using nothing but the words in the title. He could've done something along the lines of *Chairman of the Board of _______* and inserted something derogatory (Chairman of the Board of Empty Theaters), but that adds words, which we would like to avoid. Instead he'd like to make a play using the existing words. Chairman is a fairly specific term, without any other meanings or homonyms, so it's not an easy word to use in wordplay. However, board has many meanings, and by running through them in his head MacDonald was able to find the perfect usage.

You can see how by analyzing the context, MacDonald is able to narrow down his focus and determine the type of joke to make before he finds the actual joke. This saves precious time and is the reason that comedians are able to come up with barbs like this in seemingly no time flat.

The trick to these reactive gems is to analyze your situation and quickly find jokes. You do this by examining the context and using that to narrow down the avenues you can use for jokes. In both situations our witty champions took what was given to them and used that as the setup for their jokes. One of the hardest things about wit is knowing what to joke about, but by using the environment as a set up you immediately limit your options and make it much more manageable. Churchill knew that he had to defend himself and launch a counterattack, but he also know the woman was right. So, he used that information, along with the generally accepted unattractiveness of the target to quickly decide which tools he could use to craft the joke. Norm knew that he had to attack the title of the movie, so he instantly knew what he was working with. He had three words to use to make the joke, so all he had to examine were those words. Instantly recognizing the tools you have to work with is the main step in becoming reactively witty. From there you find the best joke you can with those tools. It takes years of practice, but the theory is straightforward.

Proactive

Proactive wit is creating a witty thought when time is not a factor. Most often you'd see it in writing, or in a formal response that has been crafted. People are not under the impression that the remark is off the cuff, and because of that the threshold for what is clever enough to be witty is much higher. Since timing is removed, the quickness is gone and it's much higher to get a reaction from people. But since you have ample time to prepare, you should be able to get the wording just right.

Here are a couple of examples:

> *"Tell him I was too fucking busy-- or vice versa."*
> *Dorothy Parker, when asked to explain to her*
> *editor why she was late on her deadlines.*

Dorothy Parker's writing is full of beautifully witty phrases and ideas, and she was ruthless. Here she shows one of the greatest advantages of witty writing – because you're not expecting a laugh, you don't need people to get it immediately. This joke is exceedingly clever, chances are good that once you read it you have to go back and re-read the first part to appreciate it. In reactive wit this isn't great, because you want a reaction. You'd have to make it more obvious. But since it's in writing, you can be more obtuse in your wording.
When being proactively witty it's important to realize that your first impulse isn't going to be perfect. You want to take your time and examine your response and try to add layers. Parker could have made the joke more obvious – *Tell him I was too fucking busy, or too busy fucking!* – and a listening audience would have gotten it immediately. But she took the time to obscure away the punchline, which makes it much cleverer.

Also, by changing the last line, she made the retort sound substantially less vulgar. This is a sneaky little trick to appearing clever and witty – hide your smut. By saying something that is taboo in a way that isn't, you make the audience think the taboo thing themselves. And that connection to something naughty always makes us laugh.

> *I did not attend his funeral, but I sent a nice letter*
> *saying I approved of it. – Mark Twain*

On a similar level to hiding your smut, you can also seem

exceedingly witty by saying something mean but making it sound nice. This quote, to me, is the epitome of that. On first read it sounds like a positive message, but after you think about it you realize that it was an insult. This is a real old timey way to word it, but it's pretty easy to see a modern equivalent. *You've got to be the smartest dumb guy I know,* for example.

A lot of proactive wit is finding ways to say what you want to say in a roundabout way. You want to start from the literal, and then work your way backwards a few layers until what you're actually saying is obscured, and the audience needs to do a bit of work to get there. It's like a mystery novel: the author starts at the end and works backwards. It's obvious to him, but to the reader it seems exceedingly clever. By murder-mysterying what you're trying to say, you can start to get in the habit of writing things in a clever way.

Train Your Brain
Brevity is the soul of wit

One thing you'll notice from all the examples of wit that I've shown is that they're all short and snappy. To be truly witty you need to get your point across in as few words as possible.

To practice that, take these verbose responses and re-write them with as few words as possible:

Example:
- *No thanks. I don't want to do that, it sounds like a terrible activity that I wouldn't enjoy so I will not partake*
- **I'd rather die twice**

Now it's your turn:

- *Yeah, you think that's what I'm like but in actuality you posses the qualities that you are mocking.*
- *I don't think you're making the wisest decisions here, perhaps you should rethink your approach.*
- *I'm pretty sure most of the people present in this establishment are not the sort of folk that we would enjoy hanging out with*
- *I have no intention of finishing that anytime soon, so please discontinue to ask about its progress as frankly it's annoying.*

Part 2: Practically Funny

I've thrown a lot of concepts and ideas at you so far and while I know not all of them are going to stick, I hope a few of the key ones do. If nothing else, I hope that you're always thinking about context, surprise, and expectation. The rest will come with practice. And that is what the second half of this book is going to focus on – how to put these funny techniques to work. I've given you some examples in the first half, but from this point on we'll be focused on how exactly to make people laugh.

I'll first go through some general concepts that apply no matter who you're trying to entertain. I will do my best to give you the most real-world scenarios that I can so that you can start practicing right away. There are certain hobbies and practices that funny people do without even thinking about it, and in time you will also.

I'll then dive deeper into more specific situations. Specifically, the three main areas of life: love, friendship, and work. I'll go through each area and give you specific tips to use humor to your advantage. Because even if you are funny, if you're not the right funny for the workplace, it's not an advantage. If you're not the kind of funny that draws people to you, it's not going to help you. Some of the funniest people in the world are people you would never want to be around. You don't want to be that kind of funny. I'll show you the tricks that I've learned to make life easier with humor.

Let's get into it.

Chapter 7 – Generally Funny

In this section we will go over some concepts that are key to making people laugh in all situations. I'll explain the practical mindset that you need to have when you're approaching a joke, and the way of thinking that allows you to not just be funny, but to be versatile. To be funny in a way that is going to improve your life, you want to make sure that you can interact with anyone. If you can only make one type of person laugh, you're going to be very limited in the type of connections you can make. So here are some techniques that you'll need to master to be universally funny.

7.1 Empathy

The reason a lot of people aren't funny is the same reason that a lot of people aren't good at dating: they're too into themselves. If you're not paying attention to the wants and needs of the other person, it's not going to be successful. Too many people, funny people even, only think about what makes them laugh. They feel like if they find it funny, other people have to as well, and if they don't, they're wrong. In stand-up comedy the guidance is to find your own unique voice and what makes you funny, and that's all well and good if your goal is to get on stage and entertain strangers. But if the point is to make yourself more likeable and engaging, your focus must be on what your audience enjoys.

Audience is a dumb word to use, but all I mean by it is whoever it is you are trying to make laugh. It could be one person, it could be a couple of people, or it could be a group. And your audience could change moment to moment, but whoever you want to make laugh in that moment is the first thing you need to establish. Since humor is subjective, your approach depends on the mentality of your audience. This is true from a one-on-one conversation all the way up to movies and plays.

I got taught this firsthand when I got my first real break, I got a job writing for the CBC's *This Hour Has 22 Minutes*. At first it was frustrating. I kept submitting things that I thought were very funny, but it would never make it into the show. Finally, someone pulled me into an office and explained to me that while the material I submitted might be funny to me, it's not funny to the demographic that watches the show. I was taken aback. To be frank, I had never for a second thought about who watched the show. I know that sounds stupid, but I didn't know anyone personally who watched it, so as far as I knew no one was watching. Turns out people were! And the average viewer, the person who I was meant to be entertaining, was a 41 year old woman who lived in rural Saskatchewan. I was a 24 year old man living in Halifax, who couldn't even picture rural Saskatchewan and thought 41 was ancient. How was I supposed to know what some old farmer's wife wanted to hear?

I learned a little secret that year, and I'll share it with you. **Listen to people**. I know that's not really a secret, but almost none of us do it. People are boring, and they're always talking about things that aren't me. But the first step towards understanding what a person finds funny is understanding their perspective on life, and the only way to do that is to listen to them. I mean, you could cut their skin off and try to live their life, but I feel like that would give you a pretty skewed vision. The point is I started to actively seek out the opinions of 41-year-old women. I'd check out entertainment aimed at that group, look at their social media, basically just be a big old creep. And you know what? I started to get a sense for what made them laugh. It isn't necessarily what would make me laugh, but I could see something and appreciate how it would make them laugh.

And that's the first step: pay attention to your audience. When we talked about context earlier we said being aware of your audience's views and experiences is key to connecting with them, and listening to them is the best way to do that. Ask them questions about their lives and pay attention to the answers. Don't be a creep, but try to remember key things about them.

If that isn't psychobabble enough, to be a truly funny, truly connected person you have to go further than just listen. You really have to empathize with people. The better you can see things from other people's perspective the better you are able to properly contextualize your jokes. You almost want to build a character profile for each person you interact with. Even if you've just met them, start collecting information. Be careful when you're doing so, and **don't make assumptions.** The whole point is to see things from their point of view, and any assumptions you make will have your opinion bleed into them. Instead, incorporate facts and opinions that they have directly told you, regardless of what you have observed on your own. This is important, because of someone tells you they hate sour cream and onion chips, that's the way they want to be perceived. Doesn't matter if you've seen them greedily devour a bag of SC&O before, if you joke about something different than what they've said, it makes them like you less. It's fine to do that with close friends, but if you are trying to make someone like you, stick to the facts as they present them.

Train your brain
Exploiting Empathy

You probably hated the lateral thinking exercises we looked at early, but here's where that work pays off. More often than not, you're only going to know a limited set of facts about the person you're trying to make laugh. To get as much mileage as possible out of those facts, you need to learn to make them funny in every way possible. If, for example, I know a guy who's really into NASCAR then I want to have a new NASCAR joke every time I see him.

In order to do that, you have to think about NASCAR from as many angles as possible. Research the topic and find as many jokes about NASCAR as you can. I'll get you started:

- *You think the climate change people will ever shut down NASCAR? I mean, it's basically dudes t-bagging mother nature for 500 miles.*
- *I mean this in the least disrespectful way possible: couldn't they cock the steering wheel a little and put a rock on the gas pedal and do just as well?*
- *I didn't realize NASCAR was an acronym. Legitimately I thought it was just a redneck accent saying 'Nice Car'.*

Add as many NASCAR jokes as you can to the list. The more you write, the more you have at the ready for when you need them.

Basically, when you think of someone, you should be able to pull up the information like:

Ashley
From: Vancouver, BC
Job: Teacher
Relation to me: acquaintance
Likes: Dogs, The Office (particularly Dwight), cycling
Hates: Football, Trump, Misogyny
Beliefs: Strong feminist, pro-choice, votes liberal
Relationship status: Engaged (recent)
Misc: travelled to India recently, trying for a child,
Laughs at: stories about animals, puns, mild teasing
Doesn't laugh at: Mean spirited teasing, sarcasm, "dirty" humor

*Face created by thispersondoesnotexist.com, and as such, doesn't exist

This is the information that you want to try to build your laughs from, because people are infinitely more likely to laugh at something they agree with than something that challenges their views. Ashley loves dogs, so if I try to make jokes about how awful dogs are, she's not likely to be on board. She's pro-choice, so mild jokes that are poking fun at pro-lifers are likely to get a laugh. We can use these facts and beliefs to build jokes that we know will connect with our audience.

And beyond just joking, we can use this information to build conversations that resonate with our audience and create a fertile breeding ground for laughter. For instance, I know that Ashley travelled to India recently, so before I see talk to her I can think of leading questions about India. I know Ashley doesn't like mean spirited humor, so I try to pick non-insulting directions to go down. It takes some practice in lateral thinking, but if you sit down and brainstorm India you can think of a lot of questions you can ask that could be amusing. Let's try that as an example.

My Goal: Funny and interesting conversation about India with Ashley, using the above information.

With my goal defined, I now have to brainstorm about India to think of topics that could be rich with humor. Here's what I think of (good and bad, we don't want to censor at this point) when I think of India, and how I analyze each idea to decide what I should talk about. This all happens very quickly and sometimes subconsciously, but the idea is to narrow down your scope so that you can come up with interesting ideas rapidly.

Basically, one of the problems with being funny is that there are an infinite number of things to make jokes about, and it can be difficult to decide what to say. By using what we know about our audience as a filter, we can sort through our ideas before we waste too much time thinking about them. *Travelled to India recently* is a random example I made up so that I could take you through my filter process. Here are some of the things, good and bad, that I think of when I think of India. Not all of these are accurate or proper to talk about, but that's part of the filtering process. Part of lateral thinking is letting your brain wander, and then filtering the good ideas from the bad:

- **Taj Mahal** – I know the Taj Mahal exists, I *believe* it was built by an Emperor for his wife. That is the extent of my Taj Mahal knowledge, I don't really have a wealth of jokes or follow up questions.
- **Tigers** – I think of Tigers when I think of India, but I have no idea why. If I'm honest with myself, I don't know if there are still tigers there, or if there ever were. I don't want Ashley to think I'm dumb, so I'll avoid this altogether.
- **Ghandhi** – ever since I read an article about him forcing young girls to sleep in his bed, I have a hard time joking

about Ghandhi in a not mean way. Ashley doesn't like that kind of thing, so we can't use this

- **Hygiene** – I think a lot of us entitled westerners have heard some questionable stories about the hygiene in India, and the taboo nature of the subject could lead to some funny moments. However, if you're not careful with your wording you could look very ignorant. Ashley is only an acquaintance, and in general isn't a fan of dirty ideas, so while it might interest me, I know my audience won't appreciate it, so I'd avoid this.

- **Bollywood** – I find Bollywood fascinating, just not to the point that I'll watch it. But if I'm on a plane and someone is watching it in front of me I will spend a lot of time looking at it. I think there is a lot to talk about here, and a lot of it could be funny, but if I look at it objectively, I might come across as disrespectful to Bollywood. Since I don't know Ashley's position on Bollywood I want to hold back so I don't risk offending her. However I'll keep my ideas on this topic at the ready in case it comes up.

- **Arranged Marriage** – I know that arranged marriages are quite common in India, and with Ashley getting married soon this is a very relevant topic. Also, I know that Ashley is a very vocal feminist and she's likely to be against the concept. This is a great position to be in, because if you know someone passionately dislikes something it gives you the greenlight to make fun of it. However I also realize that it's a difficult thing to segue to naturally. *Hey! I heard you were in India. How about those arranged marriages?* Looking at it objectively, it feels a bit forced. But I feel like this is by far my best idea, so I really want to find a way to use it.

So I've found my goal topic: arranged marriage. I think Ashley will connect very strongly with it, it's a topic with a lot of depth. However, I also know it's an awkward topic to segue into, so I now have two goals:

1) Find a way to start a conversation about Ashley's trip to India that I know will lead us to talk about arranged marriage.
2) Think of some funny jokes about arranged marriage.

The way we solve step one is to find something that is in some way connected to both arranged marriage and India in such a way that I can bring it up organically, and then segue the conversation to arranged marriage myself. This way, I can be sure we end on the topic I want. To do this I can walk my way back through my ideas on India and see if I can find one that links to marriage. Luckily, I don't have to look very far: The Taj Mahal! It was built by an emperor for his wife. And *Did you go to the Taj Mahal?* is a very reasonable opening question for someone who just got back from India. Then, regardless of her answer, I can move the conversation along by saying something to the effect of: *It's so beautiful, I heard it was built as a gift for his wife. He must have loved her an awful lot, that's one hell of a good advertisement for arranged marriage.*

I say that *knowing* that Ashley will disagree with the statement. I also disagree with the statement, but this is a little advanced trick. By saying something I know will get her angry, I can then abandon my position and join her in being angry at arranged marriage. *I was joking, I agree, I can't believe they do that!* Now we're both on the same team angry at a common target that isn't present, and this is a fantastic place to be. Now we can both attack arranged marriage and laugh at it together, bringing us closer and building trust and likeability between us. Now all we have to do is think of funny things about arranged marriage.

Thinking of funny jokes about a topic is like the above process – you have to sit down and brainstorm ideas about the topic. For me, the easiest way to do this is to think of different aspects of the topic, and then try to find the funny in those. I find that my main topic is often a bit daunting to look at as a whole, and by breaking it down to smaller ideas I not only get more funny premises, I also ask more interesting questions. Most people will ask the same surface level questions, so by taking the extra time to dissect you are setting yourself apart and making yourself more interesting.

Learning how to break it down into pieces and knowing which ones are going to be funny takes some practice. There are no rules as to what the pieces are, you just want to find any aspect or angle on arranged marriage that you think will connect with your audience. Here's how I would break down *arranged marriage*:

- *Parent's bad taste* – The first thing that jumps out at me is that my parents and I do not have the same taste in anything. They'd pick a partner that would be awful for me but they would love. In my judgement this is a funny premise, and it is a non-offensive idea. The victims in the joke are my relationship with my parents and arranged marriage, neither of which should offend my audience. So now I just need to figure out how to word it.

  My gut instinct is usually to use analogies where I can, because to me it is a concise, funny way to get an idea across. So I try to think of a way to express how my parents taste is different than mine. One obvious way that is very relatable is clothing: very few people have the same style as their parents. And the trivialness of clothing choice provides a good surprise against the seriousness of arranged marriage.

  Now that I have my method of humor and the meat for my analogy, I play with the words in my head until I find a way to hide my full reveal until the end. The finished product comes out something like this:

I can't imagine having my parents choose my wife, I wouldn't even let my parents choose my outfit.
It's much less funny when you see the way the sausage is made, but if it appears off the cuff, it will catch people off guard and likely get a laugh.

- *Dowry* – The concept of a dowry has always been bizarre to me, and there are a number of funny questions/ideas about it. But I need to keep in mind the audience. I want to ensure that whatever jokes I make about a dowry are attacking the concept of arranged marriage and not the victims of the practice. It makes it more challenging, but at the same time it eliminates options so it helps get to your jokes quicker.

Looking at the idea of dowry through the filter of Ashley's context allows me to see the dog in the room: the dowry system is reversed here. In an arranged marriage, the bride's family must pay the husband's family, however in our system, the husband has to buy a ring for the wife. It's a funny idea, but stepping back and looking at it objectively it's possible to say it in such a way that it is offensive. We don't want to make Ashley feel guilty for the money spent on the ring. So instead, we focus on her feminist ideals and try to portray the idea in a feminist light. We can frame it as though it was a positive feminist breakthrough and that men are almost the victim. This is done with a tone of irony so that Ashley knows I'm not serious. After massaging the wording a bit we get something like this:

It's insane that the bride's family has to pay a dowry. I don't know how you did it but women really flipped that on us here. Not only do we not get a dowry, we have to buy a big stupid expensive ring.

- *Divorce* – We all know that one of the biggest parts of marriage is divorce, so that leads me to wonder if arranged marriages suffer the same fate. There's nothing inherently funny about the divorce of an arranged marriage, until you bounce the words around in your head enough to come up with *Arranged Divorce*. Which plays into Ashley's context very well, and quite frankly is a hilarious concept.

  Because *arranged divorce* is a clever wordplay-ish type phrase, I feel that it's strong enough to be a punchline on its own. And then the imagine it conjures up, which for me is two sets of parents coming together to decide that they've had enough of their kids dumb marriage and making them get a divorce, can almost be used as a tag.

  So I would open by asking (with ironic innocence) *If they get an arranged marriage, do they also have to get an arranged divorce?* The hope is that I will get a laugh from this idea alone as everyone takes a moment to ponder it. I can then offer up my fun imagery of two sets of parents having enough of their kids marriage as an additional joke.

- *Ceremony* – I can only imagine that the ceremony for an arranged marriage in India is a butt-ton different than the ceremonies that happen here in the western world. But I also know that Ashley has been raised in North America and therefore is more familiar with the customs there. So I envision a Western ceremony for an arranged marriage as I know it plays into her context. One of the most iconic parts of a Western marriage is the moment when the official asks *do you take this person to be your lawfully wedded blah blah*. If you think about that for an arranged marriage it's a bit ironic to ask, because clearly they don't have a choice. That's the whole premise of the arranged marriage.

In essence, the dog I want to show them is that you can't have one of our most well known customs as part of an arranged marriage ceremony. There's nothing more we really need to do with it, as the idea is very clear. All we need to do is word it in such a way that all of the information is there and the surprise is at the end. Saying it out loud a few times leads me to this:

I've never been to an arranged marriage, but I bet they skip the part where they ask "Do you take this person", since, you know, they don't have a choice.

If it was in writing, I would stop at "..take this person" and allow the reader to figure it out on their own to get that *aha!* moment. But experience has taught me to add the last part to give the audience the full information. It's difficult for any audience to get the joke quick enough to laugh without the full information. They will likely still find it funny, but if you want them to physically laugh, you have to hold their hand sometimes.

You can see that by analyzing the context of our audience and doing some prep work, we have been able to quickly put together the backbone of an interesting conversation. We honed in on a fact we know about Ashley (she's recently been to India), analyzed it to find an interesting subtopic (arranged marriage), created a natural conversation segue to our topic (by using the Taj Mahal), and created no less than 4 interesting, funny takes on the topic that we have pre-filtered through Ashley's context and believe she will enjoy.

By taking the time to prepare we can fly through a conversation with Ashley and show her that we are funny, interesting, and well aligned with her world view. She doesn't know that we've pre-prepared these ideas, to her it seems as though we are naturally wonderful conversationalists. This extra work is what makes funny people consistently funny and likeable. Focusing on the audience ensure that you are consistent with their world view which in turns makes them remember you as a funny, likeable person.

Mull it Over
An analogy for empathy

Earlier in the book I compared creating jokes to cooking a meal, and it's useful to keep that in mind when you're thinking about empathy. Because a person's sense of humor is a bit like their taste in food. If someone hates eggs (I'm someone), it doesn't matter how you prepare the eggs, that person isn't going to like it. Sure, you might be able to trick them into enjoying eggs if they're hidden within the dish, but it takes a lot of work.

The same is true with humor. If someone hates jokes about sex or violence or any topic, it doesn't matter how funny your jokes is about it, they aren't going to enjoy it. By paying attention to the person, you can learn what they like and what they don't like and use that to cook up some beautiful jokes.

Remember: **you** are trying to make **them** laugh. You have to go to them, not the other way around.

7.2 Self Awareness

Here are two rules that I hold to be true:

1. No matter how funny you are, a whole bunch of people are still going to find you unfunny.
2. No matter how funny you're being, people will get tired of it.

I believe these to be laws of the universe, and we need to respect these laws if we want to achieve our goals of being funny and likeable. But what do they mean in a practical sense?

Every single one of you has watched a video that you thought was the funniest thing ever, only to show it to a friend who is unimpressed. I've said it a bunch but it's just so important, humour is subjective. There's nothing that everyone finds funny. Here's a handy little chart to help explain it:

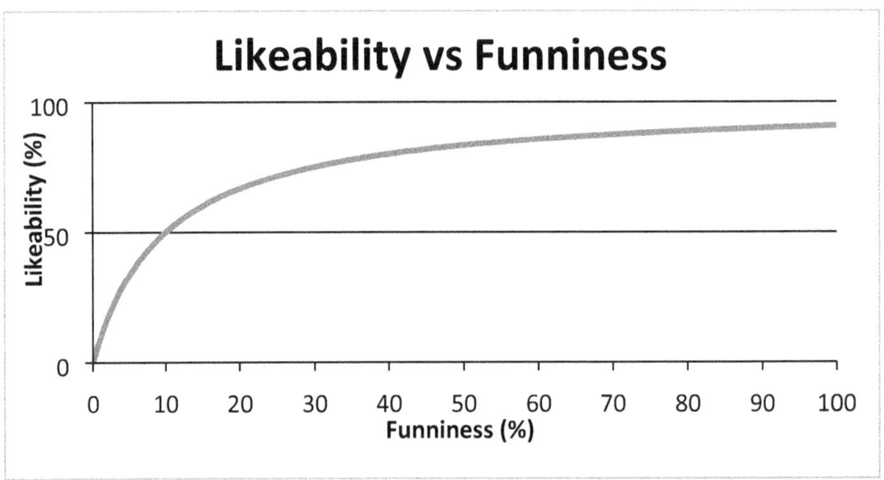

Even if you're the funniest person alive, there are people who just won't like you. If you're trying to be funny to someone, and they aren't on board, you might just have to shut the hell up already. You're not going to convince someone who doesn't think you're funny that you are. Even if you do everything right. Even if you understand them and their context, they just flat out don't find you funny. You have to accept that and move on. Don't keep trying, it just makes it worse.

It's up to you to catch this, and it isn't always obvious. Sometimes they'll smile at you still or laugh politely, but you need to be able to tell that it's a fake laugh. If you're not good at telling the difference, get on YouTube and start doing some research. Trying to force funny onto an unwilling audience is the quickest way to have them hate you. And if they hate you, they could spread that opinion to others. And if others hear that you're annoyingly unfunny before they even meet you, there's a pretty good chance they're going to find you unfunny.

To this day it hurts when people find me unfunny, so I understand the impulse to be defensive about it. Sometimes people take it personally and decide that they'll do anything to prove to them that you're funny. You have to swallow that impulse. It's nothing personal, their humor just doesn't connect with yours. One of the hardest things about being a funny person is accepting failure. Comedy is a bit like gambling, you can't win all the time. If you can't accept that, you shouldn't be trying to be funny.

When you do run into someone who just doesn't find you funny, your subconscious instinct is going to be to avoid talking to them. You want to be funny, so talking to someone who isn't on board is draining, so you'll find yourself veering away from them conversationally. Try to fight this impulse, and be extra polite to these people. The best thing you can do is to make sure that they find you nice and pleasant, if not funny. That way, they are less likely to poison the opinions of other people. It's difficult, but the more generally positive people's opinions are of you, the easier it is to make people laugh.

Comedy movies are by far the shortest genre on average. Stand up comedy, even when done in nice theatres, is still hours shorter than your standard theatrical performance. There's a reason for that: **comedy is tiring**. I mean that in a few different ways. First, the physical act of laughing is kind of exhausting. Laughing for a long period of time takes a toll on you both physically and emotionally, and at a certain point you just can't do it anymore. Your brain won't find things funny and your body is aching in those weird muscles in your abdomen.

Beyond that, watching comedy is an active experience. You have to be paying attention all the time, because jokes are easy to miss. You have to be engaged all the time or you'll miss the funny parts. It can't be a background experience like music can, it requires the audience to put in some work. If the audience isn't actively listening and thinking on their own, comedy just doesn't work. And for the audience to put forth that effort requires energy which we know is a limited resource. So it's tiring that way.

And it's also tiring because comedy relies on surprise, and it's nearly impossible to keep surprising someone ad nauseam. If you watch any sort of comedy produced by the same artist for long enough, you'll start to notice patterns. You'll become a little less surprised, and a little less entertained. Eventually, the artist runs out of surprises. It becomes tiring for both the artist and the audience, and suddenly no one is having fun anymore.

Getting a laugh is an incredible feeling, and everyone loves that high. And for most of us (myself included) the instinct is to chase that high as fast and hard as possible. What I mean practically is that if I make someone (or a group) laugh, my instinct is to tell them as many jokes as humanly possible. If I get a laugh in a group, I want to not stop. The problem with this is twofold: first, if you're rushing to try to get as many jokes out as possible, you're quality is going to suffer. You're going to start letting worse jokes fly than you normally would, because your patience is non-existent. You want those laughs now!

Obviously this is bad, because consistently putting out poor quality jokes is going to tarnish your funny person image.

But even if you are hitting homeruns all night, if you don't pick your punches, you're going to be annoying. I've seen the funniest human beings alive have people walk away from them in conversation because they come across as a self-indulgent douche. You can't have a joke for everything, or you become a joke yourself. People won't take your seriously. You want to be a person who is funny, not a sitcom character. Make sure you don't overdo it. Jokes are like frosting: you can't have a cake that is all frosting. Sure, it sounds delicious but really quickly you'll find it disgusting. Trust me, I know.

7.3 Other General Tips

Don't be the hero

One gross mistake I see a lot of attempted funny people often make is that in every story they tell, they win. And by *win* I mean they were always the smarter one, or the funnier one, or the one who came out on top. The punchlines to their story are always *and then I told him [insert hilarious thing I said]...* or *then I [did a crazy thing]...* or *...so I [some clever thing to outsmart]*. They're always Bugs Bunny to the world's Elmer Fudd.

It comes off as arrogant and insecure. Here's what I believe deep down to my core: if you're truly funny, people will tell your winning stories for you. Let other people do your bragging, because when you tell your own hero stories, people resent you a bit. If you want to connect with people and make them laugh in a way that also makes them like you, you have to be vulnerable. You're not vulnerable when you're winning; you're vulnerable when you're losing.

It's difficult to wrap your head around, but if you can tell a story where you're the butt of the joke and allow people to laugh at your pain, you can connect with them more than any cool guy story. People are flawed, and they connect with other people who are flawed. You want them to hear the cool guy stories from others, and the *aw-shucks* story from you, because then you don't look like a tool.

Don't be your own biggest fan

If we're honest with ourselves, we're all faking about 90% of our confidence. It's impossible to be confident all the time. And we all have our own little ways of compensating for that. Unfortunately, when people aren't confident with their funny, one thing they do subconsciously is laugh at their own jokes. Sometimes we see it as arrogance, but it's almost always nervousness. People are so worried that no one will laugh at their joke that they laugh pre-emptively in the subconscious hope that it will stir others to laugh.

For the love of God, don't be the first one to laugh at your own joke. Absolutely no one finds that endearing. While you're laughing, everyone else is rolling their eyes and hating your guts. I'm not saying you shouldn't laugh at your own jokes, you should definitely laugh along with your audience. Otherwise you kind of look like a psychopath. Just don't be the first to laugh. Wait until you hear the sound of *genuine* laughter before you let yourself laugh along.

Acknowledge the bomb

In the comedy world, when a joke doesn't get a laugh we call it say that it *bombed.* It happens all the time, and let me tell you, the silence is deafening. The same either has or will happen to you in conversation, and it's the worst feeling. But there is a little showbiz trick to win back the audience, and it's easy on paper but difficult on the ego. **Admit you told a bad joke**.

This isn't going to work if you're dropping bombs like the Luftwaffe, but if you have an occasional miss, let the audience know that you know that it sucked. If you tell a joke that bombs, let the pause hang for a second so everyone knows what happened, then simply saying something like *swing and a miss on that one* can get a bigger laugh than your joke ever could have. Because the tension caused by a failed joke is palpable, there's a discomfort in the room. Everyone is thinking about how you just whiffed a joke. If you cut that tension by acknowledging it, you're giving people permission to laugh at *you* instead of the joke. This completely releases the tension and allows everyone to acknowledge their feelings.

The other benefit of this little tactic is that it reassures the audience that you know what you just said wasn't funny. People know not every joke will work, but when you send out a real stinker, it makes people think *does he think that's funny?* If you don't know them very well it can make them question your sense of humor. By acknowledging it, you let them know that it was just a mistake, not a mindset.

Get a Laugh RIGHT NOW
Turn a flub into a laugh

The deafening silence following a joke that no one laughs at is a long and painful moment. All professional comedians have lines prepared to cover for jokes that don't work. You should do the same. Here are some ready-to-use savers for when you fall flat:

- Listen, they can't all be winners
- In my defense, good jokes are hard
- Not a _____ crowd hey? (fill in the blank with the topic)
- I'll show myself out
- You guys didn't like that, but trust me it's worse for me
- Hard no on that one hey?
- (if someone tries to fake laugh) no no, this is the only way I'll learn
- Look, you miss 100% of the shots you dont take
- Even though no one laughed, I want to point out that was a joke so that no one thinks I meant it

That painful moment is an opportunity. The tension it creates means that if you say anything vaguely appropriate with the right timing you can get a laugh. Cutting that tension is such a relief that you're bound to get a reaction. It takes practice to find the right lines for your personality, but seize the opportunity vacuum before someone else does!

Be a good audience

One of the absolute simplest things you can do to make people think of you as a funny person is to laugh at their jokes. If you laugh with someone, they are more likely to laugh with you back. It's that simple. Laughing at someone's jokes instantly makes them like you. Think about it, if you know someone is going to enjoy your stories, you can't wait to tell them. Be that person.

And take it a step further, when someone is trying to be funny, play along with them. Ask them leading questions and try to grow funny. I know I've poo-poo'd on Improv a bit already, but they do have some great tools. The main rule of improv is something called *Yes, and...*, and what it means is that no matter what idea your partners are throwing at you, you have to accept it and add to it. You never shoot down ideas, instead you build on them. While this works in improv, I'm not going to tell you to never shoot down ideas, because a lot of ideas are flat out stupid. But whenever possible you should try to accept. If someone is joking with you, try to go along with them. This is how you build moments.

Let me try to give you a practical example. This is a real example from my real life. I have a friend who likes to come to me with intentionally dumb ideas he comes up with, purely because he knows that I will play along. It took me a while to get to this point with him, because my gut instinct is to be a cynic. I'd only ever hear his ideas as part of a group, because he knew my instinct is to tear down. My gut doesn't say *yes, and...*, it says *no, because....* And that's how I was handling him, I would try to get laughs by mocking his ideas. And oftentimes I would. I could find a huge glaring flaw in his idea (spot the dog), point it out and get a laugh from the group.

But I started to notice that after that one laugh, that was it. Subject was over, and there would either be silence or we would need a new topic. But when I didn't have a good put down, the group would talk about the idea for a much longer time. And eventually we'd get to a point where we'd all laugh about the idea. No matter how dumb it was, if we batted it around long enough, it would become funny. And I started to realize that if I work to build up the idea instead of tear it down, I can help ensure we all consistently have a better time. And it worked to the point that now any dumb idea he thinks of he brings to me and we always have a good laugh.

Here's what I mean. This is a real idea he came to me with a few years ago.

Him: You know how tsunamis are really deadly and terrifying and they kill lots of people.
Me: Yeah
Him: You know what would make them even more deadly and terrifying?
Me: What?
Him: Imagine if the water was boiling hot!

Now you can probably see why my instinct is to tear down the idea. There are about a million reason why it's a dumb idea, and any number of them are funny. Like how the hell did the water get boiling hot? And how could it stay boiling hot without the temperature of the earth being boiling hot? And no warning or anything? Just a boiling hot tidal wave out of nowhere? If the ocean is boiling hot we've got bigger problems than tsunamis surely. There's a lot to make fun of here.

And that's the only place that my head would go for years when he would spring these ideas on me, until I inadvertently learned the rule of *yes, and...* Because while there is a hundred ways to tear down the idea, if you look at it the other way, there are also a hundred funny ways to build up the idea. Really, no matter how dumb an idea is, there are funny aspects to it. First of all, Hot tsunami is a fantastic name, it sounds like a Japanese pop band that I'm too old to enjoy. We also couldn't stop laughing at the image of a fisherman pulling up an already boiled lobster, or the idea of a beach full of people being run over by the rogue wave only to have a beach full of skeletons left in its wake. And listen, it's not that funny objectively, but in the moment where we are exploring the idea, the moment is undeniable. These are the moments you want to try to create.

Mull It Over
Accepting a bad suggestion

When someone says something real dumb trying to be funny, it can be really easy to shit all over them. It's a quick laugh, but it's a dead end. Instead, use the things you've learned to try to understand what it is that they find funny.

You may not agree with the take, but chances are at the heart of it there is something funny. It can be hard to riff on a bad joke, but if you can understand the idea behind it, you can add your own jokes based on that. That way you're not tearing down but building up.

Imitation is Flattery

Listen for phrases and wordings that make you laugh, and don't be afraid to incorporate them into your own vocabulary. The popularity of super repetitive jokes like *That's what she said* and *weird flex, but ok* can prove to you that people aren't dying for originality. I'm not saying you should copy everything you find funny, but find ways to lean on things you already know are funny to bolster conversations. The more you get comfortable saying funny things, the more confident you'll get creating your own.

These are some of the things to keep in mind to connect with a wide variety of people. The most important idea though is that the person you're trying to make laugh should be the focus. They might not find the same things funny as you do, so by understanding them as a person you can understand what makes them laugh. By focusing on what they like as opposed to what you like you not only have a better chance of making them laugh, but you also have a better chance of showing them that you're attentive and caring, which makes them like you. Being empathetically funny does way more than just make someone laugh, it makes them feel loved.

Being funny in real life takes a lot of work, but it also takes a lot of awareness. You need to be watching and listening to everything around you, and your audience. The better you understand people, the better you can make them laugh. The audience is your guide, and the audience is your judge.

Chapter 8 - Funny at work

When I was 21, I was an Electrical Engineering student at Dalhousie University, and I was in dire need of an internship. I desperately needed the money and the experience, but I knew it was going to be difficult for me to get one because I was *substantially* dumber than most of my peers. These dudes were building wind turbines for fun, there was no way any reasonable company would choose me unless they were allergic to nerd. Internship hiring went in three rounds, and after each round these companies would make job offers. Oftentimes, the best students get multiple offers, so they must make a choice. This leaves some companies out in the cold, so they re-interview again in the later rounds to find someone else. For the first two rounds of hiring, I didn't get a single interview.

It was disappointing, but not surprising. In the third and final round I finally got a single interview. It was with some awful oil company that I never wanted to work for, but on the other hand I really wanted money. This company would not normally have looked at me, but their top choices in the previous rounds all took other jobs, so they were casting a wide net. As soon as I walked into the waiting room, I knew I was never going to get this job. The whole room was filled with guys just like me, except better dressed in both clothing and grades. I was quite possibly the least qualified person interviewing for this job.

The thing about having nothing to lose is that there's nothing to be nervous about. I walked into that interview with 0 expectations, and because of that I was able to relax. And by that point in my life, I was getting pretty funny. I was about a year away from starting comedy, and I had figured out a lot of the techniques that I've described in this book. It hard brought me to the point that I was consistently funny in conversation, and people knew me as a funny person. We had been instructed on how to conduct ourselves in these interviews, and we were meant to act very proper. And because of that, I thought the interviewers might enjoy a little break from that. I was going to try to be funny. Why not? They've seen my transcript and resume. We all know that I'm the least qualified person for this job. So why go through the motions of a regular sham interview?

I got the job. They would later tell me that I seemed so confident that they had no choice but to offer me the job. *There's something about you* they said. And so, I spent 4 months working for an oil company doing menial office labor. Everyone in the office would eventually agree that I was awful at it. I was slow and inconsistent, but I was great for morale. I would make people laugh, but beyond that, I would make people feel *good*. By understanding how to create funny moments with my workmates I would make the day more tolerable. In my exit interview, my boss would go on to say:

> *I would never recommend you for this job. You're terrible at this job. But I would most certainly recommend that you come back as a manager*

By understanding the context of the work environment and exploiting that to create a funny atmosphere for my colleagues, I was able to make myself a very valuable employee. This pattern has repeated itself over and over again throughout my life. Every job I've had I've been bad at, but every single one has given me a great reference.

This isn't a brag, and it isn't difficult. In this section I'll show you how you can use the techniques in this book and the context of the work environment to make yourself indispensable. Obviously, all workplaces are different, but the concepts and principles of workplace humor are universal. With that, let's get to it.

8.1 Cover Letters

The first place that you can exploit a bit of humor to your advantage is with the cover letter. Think about it from the perspective of the employer: they're reading a ton of these things and every one of them is pompous and boring. Most jobs have a ton of applicants and each one of them are writing a cover letter, and quite frankly, they're tedious. Everyone is a very hard worker, everyone has excellent communication skills, and everyone works well independently. It's hard to avoid, but because most letters are so similar it is an excellent chance to set yourself out from the pack. Take it from someone who's read a lot of cover letters: if you stand out, you get noticed.

I know it's incredibly tempting to have a standard cover letter that you modify slightly for all applications, but I implore you: write a fresh one each time. Even if you reuse most of the same text, writing it from scratch will make it read more personalized and have a better chance to connect with the reader. But it also allows you to include jokes specifically written for this job and that proves to the reader that you care enough to not just do your research, but to mull it over in your head to the point that you can make jokes. Because joking about something shows that you've really put thought into it, and that resonates with companies.

You want to keep the jokes to a minimum, but there are a few exceptions. One is to bring up something **complimentary about the potential employer** as part of a joke. To do this, you have to research the company. For the sake of the letter, you want to limit your research to the company's website alone. You want to only include information that is provided by the company itself, that way you're sticking to the message that they approve. If you're taking from outside sources, you can't be sure that the information is something the company wants you to talk about.

When you're looking for a joke, you can make about the company you have to keep in mind that you're trying to be complimentary. You need to find something *positive* about the company that is also funny. I'll tell you this straight up: whatever you come up with is never going to be as funny as the negative things you'll come up with about the company. It's way easier and funnier to tear things down than it is to build things up. But the goal in this case isn't to get the biggest laugh. The goal is to compliment the company, show them you've done your research, and making them smile enough to remember you. So lower your expectations.

Being complimentary funny is an incredibly important skill because it allows you to say very nice things about the company without coming off as a kiss ass. Most applicants will be sucking up in a direct an obvious fashion, so if you are able to hide your compliment inside a joke it comes off as far more organic. The reader knows that you've given a compliment, but it feels indirect. As though the goal was the joke, and the compliment was collateral damage. This makes it seems as though they are your genuine feelings, as opposed to a direct suck up which can come off as tacky.

You want to browse the company's website with the intention of trying to understand a little more about their context. Let the tone of the site be the guide to the tone of your cover letter. If the company's site is very dry and serious, you want to tone down the humor a bit more. And if it's a little less serious seeming of a company, feel free to sprinkle in some extra ideas. You want to be just slightly funnier than whatever is on their site. If you try to be too much funnier than the people you're talking to, you risk coming off as a joke.

Once you think you have the tone of the company down, you want to find something specific to make an opening joke about. As I mentioned, you want it to be something positive, so your goal is to *spot the dog* with something positive. Find something about the company that (they seem to think) makes them special and try to find a way to work with that. I realize that sounds pretty vague, so let's go through a couple of examples.

We're like family – A lot of smaller companies like to pretend that their employees are *like family* despite the fact of this almost never the case. If you stumble upon that, you can easily reference this and make a joke by ironically taking the family concept too far. Here's a small example:

I read on your site that you treat your employees like family which is ideal. Family is the most important thing to me, and I work best in a close knit environment. Plus the more family the better, because who knows when you might need a kidney.

It's not a great joke but it shows that you've read their site closely and put some thought into the work environment. And by peppering in things like this you can stand out to the reader.

Obscure Awards – Lots of companies will have some meaningless award that they've recently won listed on their site (or social media). An easy reference to that can work as an introductory joke. Even something as simple as this:

I noticed that you were recently awarded the [insert garbage award here], *congratulations on the achievement. I'll admit I hadn't heard of the award before, but now that I'm aware of it I've sworn a blood oath to win it myself. Really, you'll be better off hiring me so that I'm not competing against you.*

Notice that, again, it's not much of a joke. But the ironic overconfidence insinuates that you have the drive to work extra hard, and it surprises the reader a bit. This is enough to make them pay attention to the rest of the letter.

The other type of joke that works well in cover letters is to be **complimentary toward yourself.** This is most easily done when describing your past accomplishments or your interest in the job. The way these jokes work is that they read as though they are self depreciating, but in fact they are hidden brags. It sounds complicated but it's pretty simple.

Get a Laugh RIGHT NOW
Make a joke for a specific job

Rule of 3 can be a great way to get a laugh off a mundane question. Here are some examples.

For a computer programming job:

My love of programming is almost too much, it's a bit creepy. If programming was a person it would get a restraining order.

See how the joke reads as though it's self depreciating, but the actual message is a complimentary one about myself. This allows us to brag without making it seem like we're bragging. It's a powerful tool to seem confident without seeming pompous

For a customer service job:

I'm obsessed with helping people, I can't help but put their needs before mine. I'm worried that someday someone will ask for two kidneys and that'll be the end of me.

Again, the phrasing is consistent with something that would normally be self depreciating, but the words are actually congratulatory. By finding ways to twist your positives to sound slightly negative, you can sound both humble and funny, both traits that employers associate with intelligence.

In general, you want to keep outright jokes to a minimum. Instead try to use clever wordplay or turns of phrase that aren't outright jokes, but still read interestingly. For instance, here's a sample cover letter that I wrote for a position with a machine learning software company that happened to have a pun in its name:

To Whom it May Concern,

Thank you for taking the time to review my application. ***As a lover of both algorithms and companies with witty pun names, I feel I would be an excellent fit for the position[1].*** *I have a background in Electrical Engineering and have an excellent mind for logic and mathematics. In my previous position I was mainly charged with working on front facing web apps, and I would very much like to move towards something more mathematical.* ***My inner nerd is raging within me and clawing to get out, so for the past year I have been brushing up on my math. I've had enough of friends, so I have started taking some grad level physics courses[2]*** *online and have had to dive back into the world of calculus and statistics. Conveniently, it has rekindled my love of math and I would love the chance to combine my programming ability with my fondness for numbers.*

My strength with logic and math, combined with my decade of programming experience would make me a huge asset in this position. I believe that you will find from my CV that I have all the necessary training and education, and will prove to you on the interview tests that I am more than up to the task.

Also, I feel it is important to address something on my CV. You'll notice that I am also a stand up comedian. I've spent much of the last decade touring through North America, Europe, and the Middle East performing. For much of that time I kept a full time job that I worked remotely to great success, as I worked at comedy only at night. At that time I was based in the UK, but since then I have stepped down my live performing and am

aiming to return to full time employment. I feel it's important to address this, as you'll note that I have not been working full time for the past 2 years or so. I want to ensure you that I have kept up my skills in that time, and am moving towards giving up performing as the stress vs financial incentive has become exhausting. For reference though, if you would like to have and idea what it is that I do, here is a video:
https://www.youtube.com/watch?v=9QY_u7yFe70[3]

I hope that you give me an opportunity to show what an asset I can be in this position. Any logic or programming test you give me will prove to you that I am an exceptional candidate for the position. I hope to hear from you soon and look forward to moving forward.

Thank you for your consideration,
Peter

1. Note the small joke about puns actually means a lot. The company name was a pun based on the name of the owner, so it shows that I took the time to read the site and put that together. It also shows a bit of humor and makes the read a little bit more interesting than the others without saying much different.
2. Here is an example of a self depreciating brag to try to convince the reader more subtly that you are telling the truth.
3. Notice how this section is dry because the subject is interesting and the message is serious, so I don't feel it needs to be jazzed up and if I were to, it might take away from the point I'm trying to make. By frontloading the letter with my humor I've drawn in the reader and can ensure that they will pay attention to the rest. Showing that you know when and where is appropriate to joke is also a subtle sign of maturity to the reader.

The main thing to keep in mind with your cover letter is to take your time. No piece of writing is at its best on the first draft, edit and punch up your letter and don't send it in until you're happy with it. Remember that your cover letter is the first chance to show off your personality, so if you open it correctly it can set the proper tone for your entire working relationship.

Train Your Brain
Cover Letter

This is going to be painful, but it's the only way to get better. Search for a job you would love to have and find a posting. You're going to write a cover letter for this job.

Research the job and the company and include a joke about both, as well as a short joke about yourself.

Send it to yourself via email, but don't open it for a full week. If you read it before that you'll be too close to it. After a week, you'll have forgotten what you wrote. Open it then, read it and analyze it.

Does it read the way you intended? Do the jokes feel professional?

Rewrite and repeat the process until you're happy with it.

8.2 Interviews

Now that you've nailed your smart but funny cover letter and gotten yourself an interview, it's time to prepare. This is unequivocally the best time to show off your skills. But like everything else, it's the work you put in beforehand that decides how you'll perform. I hope you can appreciate that how to ace a job interview is way outside the scope of this book, so while being funny will undeniably help you, it's not magic. If you're terrible at interviews already, this won't make you great. What being funny will do is give the chance to stand out from the crowd. To be remembered. If you're answers are terrible but funny, you'll simply be remembered as *that funny dude who we'd never ever hire.* As such, step one is to get your interview skills to a reasonable level.

Jokes within an interview are very different than jokes anywhere else. Your main objective isn't to get laughs, it's to get the job. You need your response to not just be funny, but also be a genuine answer to the question. Basically, you can't tell a joke for the sake of a joke. The joke has to be hidden within your actual answer. It's a lot more work, but it also gives you the freedom to show off more aspects of your personality and achievements.

We'll go through a bunch of examples in a minute to show you what I mean, but before that, let's look at a few things you need to keep in mind:

Context

If you've taken nothing from this book so far, I hope it's the importance of context. I've rambled on forever about understanding the audience's context and building jokes around that, but in an interview you're unlikely to know anything about your audience. Instead, you're going to have to play it safe and rely on the context provided by the business. Like above, that means doing some research. Check their website, check their social media, and try to get a feel for the company. You want to make sure that whatever you're going to say matches up with the forward-facing image of that company. What I mean by that is the jokes you can make during an interview with a Christian Bookstore are of a very different tone than the jokes you can make while interviewing to be a Strip Club DJ. While you don't know the context of the actual person giving the interview, they are acting as a representative of the company, so the context put forth by the company is the context of the audience in this case.

Ad-Libbing

Unless you're very confident in your improv reactionary ability, I'd suggest you stick mainly to pre-prepared jokes so you can be sure you don't say something offensive. Remember that *offensive* is different to everyone, and in a work environment it's way too easy to upset someone. Even if you're a pro, firing off funny lines in the proper context during a job interview has a high degree of difficulty. And even if you don't say something offensive, the chances are incredibly high that you will say something that isn't funny. Normally this isn't a big deal, but in an interview, you want to be perfect. A real stinker during an interview isn't just a bad joke, it's an awkward moment. You never forget awkward moments. That's not how you want the interviewer to remember you. Do yourself a favour and sit on the urge to improv during the interview. Save it for your friends afterwards.

Question Time

We all know that taking the time to properly prepare for an interview is incredibly important, and preparing your jokes ahead of time is no different. In most cases you have days or even weeks to prepare for an interview, so there is no excuse not to walk in with your witty *top of your head* remarks prepared. What you want to do is research and brainstorm and come up with as many possible questions as possible that you may get asked (lateral thinking strikes again). And then you want to come up with interesting answers that will entertain and inform your audience. Your mindset here has to be a bit different than some of the techniques we talked about earlier, because in this case you don't want the question to work as the setup. You don't want to respond to an interviewer's questions with a zinger, because if you do that often it will feel as though you're not taking it seriously. Also, a snappy answer than requires you to pause, make it clear you're joking, and then reset with an actual answer. This works great in conversation, but in an interview it's an awkward rhythm. It's a lot more complicated, but you want your answers to be complete setups and punchlines in themselves. What I mean is don't do this:

> **Interviewer:** So what would you consider to be your biggest weakness?
> **You:** (pauses)The inability to quickly and precisely name my biggest weakness.

It's a funny answer, but the interviewer is left feeling like the butt of a joke. You see how we took his question and changed it into a setup that we delivered a punchline to. This can be great in regular conversation, but at an interview the context is all wrong. No one wants to have their serious questions answered with disrespect, so instead you must hide the joke within your actual answer. You have to respond in a longer format that allow you to get across useful information, but also slip in something funny.

There are several ways that you can do this properly, and we'll go through a few as we answer a few sample questions to give you an idea of the type of answers I would use.

What is your biggest weakness?

Instead of using the question as a punchline like in the example above, you want to instead think of your actual answer and then insert a joke into it. So the first step is to think of your actual answer. Again, how to properly answer interview questions is outside the side of this scope but here's one thing I do know: lie. There's no reason not to lie. Don't tell them your actual weakness, make something up that seems reasonable.

The first technique we'll show is to use an **analogy**. It's an easy way to

> *My biggest weakness is that I can get a little too close to my work. I put so much of myself into it that I get attached. Every time I hand a project off to a client I feel like how a mother cat must feel giving up its kittens. I know it's right, but it kills me because it's a little part of me.*

See that's a big old crock of shit. But it's a strength presented as a weakness with a bit of a joke slipped in. Remember your jokes don't have to be killer, just enough to keep you interesting. This one presents a positive image designed to invoke likability and drive home my passion for my work.

Notice how I start by answering the question directly. This shows respect to the interviewer. The funny part is both set up and delivered in the sentences explaining the answer. By doing it this way I have complete control over the humor, and I can ensure that it is set up properly to present me in the proper light.

An analogy is simple enough to prepare when you have the time, especially given the context and conditions you have to work with. But it does take those lateral thinking skills. In this case, I first came up with my weakness: *I get too attached to my work.* So *too attached* is my starting point. I brainstorm – what are some other examples of things that are too attached? Here are other options that I had, and reasons I rejected them:

- *Like a dog with a bone* – too cliché, slightly destructive imagery

- *I'm like a tick on a deer, I can't get in deep enough* – unsettling, negative imagery

- *I get a bit like Golem with my projects, their my precious* – if the interviewer doesn't know or doesn't like Lord of the Rings I'll look real stupid

- *Have you seen the overly attached girlfriend meme? That's me with my projects* – Again, a reference that could easily be a miss. We don't want misses when we have time to prepare.

By allowing myself to explore a bunch of options I am able to narrow down on the best choice for my situation. It may not be the funniest, but I'm not looking for the biggest laugh here. I'm looking for a way to make myself seem likeable, smart, and funny in that order. It takes a lot of restraint to not go for the best jokes, but being funny in real life is all about making the right choices.

Mull it over
Interview Joke Topics

In the first half of the book, we talked about how External Factors can be more influential over laughter than anything else, and job interviews are an excellent example. There is an expectation of formality from both sides that renders a lot of humor inappropriate. Because of this, you want to prepare jokes ahead of time. Freewheeling in an interview, as I mentioned, is very dangerous. Here are some topics you can prepare jokes for, and why they help

- **Industry**: You must know about the industry to joke about it. Inside jokes shows off your knowledge.
- **Company**: shows you researched the company and care about the position
- **Previous job**: Only say nice things about your job, but you can joke about why you were a bad fit. Shows humility and politeness. Negative jokes about your old job is a bad look.
- **Current events:** shows you keep up to date and are knowledgeable about world events. Make sure it's an event everyone knows about. If you're referencing some obscure event, you'll look like a loser.
- **Self:** you can make fun of yourself as long as it's done by framing a weakness as a strength. *I work so hard it hurts my personal life* sort of idea. It allows you to bring forth a strength organically.

Sticking to these topics ensure that both you and the interviewer have the proper context

What is your biggest strength?

Ostensibly, this question is pretty much the same as the last one, except we don't need the stupid step of hiding our strength as a weakness. The technique we'll use to make it funny is a great one to make yourself seem more likeable and relatable to the interviewer. And that is to tack on a **personal anecdote** in which you are the butt of the joke. I'm going include my girlfriend because that shows some stability and commitment, and having a partner makes you come across as more likeable.

It's important to remember that these anecdotes don't have to even kind of be true. No one is ever going to fact check a two-line story in an interview, so feel free to make up something that happens to be perfect for the situation. Just don't do that for every answer. If you have a convenient personal story for every question that arises, you're going to start to seem like you're full of shit. Because you are.

My personal go-to choice for these stories is to create a scenario where a loved one is getting the better of me. It's a subtle thing, but it shows a great amount of humility. If you're comfortable telling stories in which you are the butt, and you can do it with dignity, it comes across as confidence. It shows that you don't feel like you must misrepresent yourself, you're confident enough in who you are that you can tell the truth even if you end up being laughed at. It also implies a level of trust and love between you and your partner that you have the kind of relationship where they can tease you and it is a positive experience. So, I choose to tell a story where my girlfriend makes fun of me. All of this is made up, but the interviewer doesn't know that.

Here's my answer:

> *My biggest strength is that once I get my mind set on a task, I have to get it done. Once I sink my teeth into something I will skip eating and sleeping and bathing in order to make a deadline. It drives my girlfriend crazy, she calls me a stink*

mule

It's designed to make the interviewer think of you as a crazy hard worker, but also someone with both a close relationship and a good sense of humor. It's not exceptionally funny but given the ultra serious environment it is enough to relax the mood and create a moment between me and the interviewer. I've opened up to them on a personal level, and that breeds closeness. It's also an incredibly safe joke that won't offend anyone, and because it isn't a real *jokey-joke* kind of punchline it isn't awkward if it doesn't get a laugh. All these things make the personal anecdote an excellent choice for interview jokes.

Where do you see yourself in 5 years?

I've always hated this question. What kind of boring creep knows what they're going to be doing in 5 years? I'm assuming interviewers are asking this to check to see if you're looking for long term employment so that they don't invest in you if you're just going to leave in a year. I usually try to give an answer that implies that I'm looking for a long-term commitment, and then I'll add on to that. At the time of writing this Covid-19 is still ravaging the world and Trump seems intent on setting the world on fire.

In this example I will use current events to make a small joke that helps drive home my point of desired stability. I'm going to use **hyperbole** to overstate the **current events** and try to get a laugh that way.

I don't want to be an obvious suck up and say that I see myself at this company in 5 years, because that's what a lot of people will say. Also, that really gives the company the power. I want to be a bit vaguer while still implying that I'm looking to commit to a place for a long time. I don't want to seem desperate, but I do want to show that I'm not flighty.

> *With everything that is going on right now who can say if the Earth is even going to exist in 5 years? There could be an alien attack or a nuclear war or the return of the dinosaurs... At this point nothing is off the table. What I'm looking for is a bit of stability. I'm looking to find myself a job that I like that I can focus on and throw myself into and use as a bit of a rock in this storm. I'm hoping that this is the place.*

In this case, because I don't have a direct answer, I'm putting my justification (including the humor) before the actual answer. That is because in this case the answer requires some explanation beforehand. The structure is pretty much the same, except the funny part is at the start.

Using current events is good **if** the events are such that you are confident you and the interviewer agree. In the example I'm using the entire world is concerned about the effect both the virus and Trump will have on the world, so unless I run into a *Covid is a scam* conspiracy theorist, I should be safe (And I if I do run into a conspiracy nut I'm not in a hurry to work for him anyway). This way I create likeability by using statements I know the interviewer will agree with. This creates our shared context, and by adding just a bit of hyperbole and manufactured excitement/tension I can exploit the *Us vs. Them* sense a common foe gives us. This brings us closer together and makes it more likely to get a chuckle.

Any sort of shared context in current events can be exploited to build this closeness, as long as you're sure that you are both in agreement. When you're doing your research, you should be able to glean the company's stance on current topics and use that to your advantage in the interview.

Out of all the candidates, why should we hire you?

They're basically asking what sets you apart from everyone else, and that could be anything. Just don't say you're funny. You never want to tell someone you're funny, you want to show them. Since this is open ended, you can list multiple qualities that could make you more qualified than the others. To me, the obvious choice in a situation like this is to use the **rule of three** that we mentioned at the start of the book. This allows you to give two solid reasons why you are the better candidate, and then a third funny one to show that you are a great energy to have around the office. I would say something like this:

> *Well, I have all the experience and education required to make me a standout candidate. Beyond the technical side, I also have the interpersonal and communication skills to make me a workplace asset. And if that isn't enough, come company picnic time, I make one hell of a potato salad.*

A nice safe joke that gets across the actual answer I want to convey, along with the message that I am a funny, likeable person that will make the workplace environment better.

Hopefully these examples give you an idea of how you can slide humor into your interviews to make a stronger, deeper connection with the interviewer. While I urge you to prepare as many questions as possible, don't make the mistake of trying to squeeze in a joke for every question. Try to pick your spots and use the jokes that you think are the best and cut the rest. It may seem like wasted work, but by focusing a lot of energy on each interview you'll end up having far less of them in the long run.

8.3 On the Job

Being funny on the job is one of the best ways to make yourself well liked among your co-workers, but if you're not careful it could get you labelled as a clown amongst management. Walking that tightrope involves knowing when to joke, which way to joke, and how to micromanage your humor depending on the people present. Basically, you want to joke with your bosses differently than you joke with your co-workers, and joke differently still when it's a mix of the two. It's important to keep in mind your goals, and on the job, it isn't to stroke your funny ego.

What I mean by that is that just like in the interview process, huge laughs shouldn't be your treasure here. I know it feels good, but by only following the laughs you're eventually going to say something to offend someone, or you'll get carried away and go too far, or you'll just flat out be annoying. Your goal is to be funny, but in a way that makes people think favourably about you. You have to maintain at least a certain level of professionalism.

With that said, let's go through some practical tips:

Co-workers

I keep saying it, but that's because it keeps being important: context is everything. With your co-workers at work, you want to keep your jokes about work until you get to know them as people. There's a good chance you don't have a lot in common with these creeps aside from work anyway, so it's the safest thing to talk about. However, joking about working is kind of a double-edged sword. If you're too negative about the job, it stops being funny and starts to bum people out. So you want work to be the butt of the joke, but not in a way that makes you seem as though you actually dislike the job[1].

1. This doesn't apply if you work at one of those places where *everyone* hates the job. If you're at one of those jobs then aggressively ripping the company could be your

best ticket in. Be careful about this though, and try to follow others' lead. You don't want to be the one person who goes too far and management needs to get rid of for 'morale purposes'.

The idea is that by exploiting the shared context of work, you can create a sense of closeness amongst your colleagues. What you want is an almost an '*us against the world*' vibe. The best way to do that is to talk about things that are specific to your job. Every job has those little quirks that you can't appreciate unless you've worked them, and that shared context is almost universally appreciated. I've spent a lot of years as a computer programmer, and I can instantly connect with another programmer by saying something like

> *If I knew how much of the job was copying and pasting google results, I wouldn't have wasted so much goddam money on a degree.*

For real though, the job is 85% searching things online. Showing I know that proves that I understand what they do and therefore a little bit about who they are. If you say it in a funny way, then it makes the connection even stronger. Every job has these things, and the more of them you can spot and relay to your co-workers in a funny way, the stronger you can build this connection. Here's an example from when I was a TV writer:

> *I always thought I'd rather be smart and ugly than dumb and pretty, but when I see their [actor's] checks compared to ours I think I'm the dumb one.*

The thing most people don't know about TV writers is that they believe that if they were better looking, they'd be famous themselves. Lord knows I do. So, by making fun of the job but lumping myself in first it reinforces the *we're in this together* feeling that brings people together. There are a ton of nuances in your job, then try to find funny ways to point them out. This is just *spotting the dog*. Because you're talking about things that your audience already agrees with your chances of success are even higher.

Train your brain
Use shared context at work

Every job and workplace have unique things about it that only your fellow employees understand – which means that it's a very powerful shared context. By making jokes about things only employees of the company will get you strengthen that bond and provide a release they can't get anywhere else.

Step 1
Identify something about your job that is unique. Is there something off about the building? Is there a crazy customer everyone knows? Is there a piece of equipment that never works?

Step 2
Write a joke specifically about the thing. *This blender is so painful to use that it hurts my soul. if I even look at my blender at home I start crying*

Step 3
Reinforce the unique shared context. *I never would've believed a cold drink store would have the world's worst blender, but this blender is so painful to use that it hurts my soul. if I even look at my blender at home I start crying*

The shared context of work allows you to get closer to people with minimum effort. The sheer catharsis of being able to joke about something that you can't joke with others about creates a wonderfully close connection.

Extrapolating out from the job itself, there are also lots of quirks specific to your company and your boss that can be exploited in the same way. Companies will always have strange rules or customs that will be different than most places. If you find them strange, chances are you co-workers will as well, and bringing them up will release that tension. It's one of the first things we talked about, saying something that everyone is thinking is a perfect way to get laughs.

Remember one of our other first rules too though: **external factors are the most important**. You're at work and while you may be friends with your co-workers, your still at work. It's great to make fun of the company and the boss, but you must be very non-malicious about it. You never want it to seem like you actually hate either, you want it to be more of an observation than an attack. For instance, if your company only stocks the absolute cheapest of coffees in the breakroom, you could joke about that in a way that makes you seem frustrated, or in an "aw shucks" kind of way. The difference is small on a per-joke level, but the more negative you are overall the more negative people will look at you. You become a drain on the workplace, and people don't bring things up because you'll shoot them down. So, if you notice things like the shitty coffee and say things like:

CEO makes millions meanwhile we're down here drinking bong water filtered through the anal scratchings of a donkey.

We're using hyperbole and imagery to really drive home the awfulness of the coffee, and it's a perfectly reasonable joke. But it's attacking the CEO directly, and the overall tone is strictly negative. So, you maybe you get a big laugh, but in the long run it's very bad for your image at the job. If you can temper that urge to be outright negative and do the extra work to mould your idea to fit the context, you can instead present it in a better light. You could say about the coffee:

I fully support the company's commitment to putting all

profits back into the product, it's clearly paying dividends, but maybe they could make a small exception and put a little into some decent coffee.

Not nearly as funny, but it's the same idea presented in a way that doesn't cast you in a negative light. See how I made sure to establish that I think positive of the company in general, and so this complaint is frivolous and for fun. This keeps the atmosphere light and maintains my image as a positive and fun energy. You want to keep the mood as positive as you can until you really get to know your co-workers as people and not just work robots. As you get closer and closer to them through these positively aimed jokes, you can slowly start to up the edge a bit more. Make sure you always miss on the safe side, but slowly letting co-workers in on the real you is key. It makes them feel special for penetrating past your work shell. You have to be very careful about the timing for this, try to make it outside of the work environment. If you're able to show a different side of your humor outside of work than at work and both are funny, you will immensely impress your co-workers. To the outside observer it takes a huge amount of intelligence to balance something like that.

Similarly, you want to be careful when joking about your boss. You might think its innocent, but your audience could think it's malicious. And something construed as insulting towards a person cuts harsher than towards a company, so you want to be even more careful about safety. It's really difficult, because most of the things you'll want to joke about with your boss are going to be negative. There are things bosses do that annoy their workers, and joking about it is cathartic, but you never know how they will be relayed to the boss themselves.

A trick I like is to use a similar technique to one we used in the *...greatest weakness* part of the interview section. There we spun our positives into negatives, but here we want to do the opposite. If you have something negative to say about your boss that is funny and you think your co-workers would appreciate, try to spin it as a positive. For instance, at an old job of mine, my very rich boss was incredibly cheap. We all wanted to talk about it, but at a new job you never know who the spies are, so you have to keep your guard up. What I wanted to say was:

> *If someone offered him eternal life for a dollar that stingy prick would offer 50 cents*

But I realize that comes across as bitter, jealous, and petty. So, I stop, and I rethink. What is a positive thing about being cheap? It's like being smart with money, and he is rich. Perhaps cheapness is the cause of it? I was finally able to broach the topic with my co-workers, and it really brought us together, by going with this:

> *The other day I started to get frustrated with how cheap he is, but then I realized how broke I am and how rich he is and thought "maybe he's onto something..."*

It's not incredibly funny, but it's a bit of self deprecation to get the ball rolling, and it frames him in a positive light. And more importantly, now that the topic had been brought up, it allowed the conversation to start, and we all ended up making jokes about it. In cases like this where everyone is hesitant to bring up a topic, a very mild joke can be the icebreaker you need to really bond.

Bosses

Joking with your boss is inherently more complicated than joking with your co-workers because your co-workers can't fire you on the spot. The power dynamic makes the waters a bit muddier, but like any sort of tension it can be exploited to your advantage. I think it goes without saying that all the rules about caution that we discussed about co-workers goes doubly for your boss. No laugh is worth tarnishing your boss's view of you. But the advantages of making your boss laugh are obvious – if the person in charge likes you then your job is safe.

Hopefully it's also obvious that you can't joke about your boss to your boss the same way you'd joke about your boss to your co-workers. You can't turn a negative into a positive about someone to their face, they'll see right through it. Instead, the best way to handle a boss at work is to be what I call **submissively funny**. What I mean by that is that in your jokes you acknowledge the boss's superiority. It's basically sucking up, but you hide it in a joke so that neither of you feel uncomfortable.

It's going to take some practice. You have to find the right balance of compliment and attack to make it feel respectful but also funny. But the idea is to choose an attribute to compliment (experience, knowledge, work ethic, success, etc) and create the joke around that. Self deprecation can work here but try to limit it to be in relation to your boss as opposed to straight up taking a dump on yourself. For instance, you can say that you're stupid *compared to your boss*, but don't just say you're stupid. Too much straight self deprecation will come across as lack of confidence, whereas comparative deprecation is more of a compliment.

Hopefully some examples will things up a bit. Here are some real examples of things I've said to bosses that have gotten laughs:

- After asking him a question and getting an answer: *You know, it'd almost be nice if you didn't know the answer for once so at least I'd know you're a human and not some cyborg or something*

  Here I've taken a compliment about how knowledgeable my boss was and worded it as a light attack. The surprise of the wording mixed with the unexpected compliment gets a laugh and builds likeability.

- On being asked what my future goals were: *I've seen how nice your house is compared to how crappy my house is, my goal is to learn what you've done and emulate that. I'm going to steal your essence. Don't let me near your wife.*

First of all, I only added the wife part because I had already built up a lot of likeability with this boss. Don't use something like that until you're sure of the boss's humour. But the first part stands on its. Particularly if you're in a beginner role at a company, complimenting your boss's success tends to go a long way. Everyone likes to hear that someone aspires to be them, so if you can say it in a way that isn't so suck-ass it makes people happy. They start to see you as a protégé or younger sibling, and they want to help you.

- On their management style: *Frankly I don't know how you deal with all of us – I only have to deal with myself and it's almost too much.*

Here's a compliment that is hidden in some relative deprecation. Notice that at no point I say that I am unable to handle my responsibilities, just that I would be unable to handle theirs. It's a small thing but it has huge implications. But beyond the mechanics of the joke, the real power lies in its perspective. The joke implies that I've taken the time to think about things from the boss's angle, and that has a powerful effect on people. It shows that you care and have empathy for their issues, and that does wonders to make someone like you.

When dealing with bosses outside of work you should keep the same angle of jokes but make your language a little less formal. When outside of the job you can also joke about other things other than work to show your boss your casual humor. You still need to be sure to vet the things you joke about though, because personal topics that cast you in a negative light will carry over to work. You want your boss to think that non-work you has the same values as work you, just with your hair let down a bit.

Get a Laugh RIGHT NOW
Crack your boss up

No one likes a suck up, but people love being complimented. By hiding your compliments in jokes and framing them from your bosses perspective, your boss sees you as an intelligent, empathetic person. And if the jokes are good, they'll think your clever on top of it. Here are some examples I've used for making my boss laugh and like me more.

- Do you ever not work? I mean, I'm always working but I barely work compared to you. What's the secret, coke?
- It's got to be weird to have to hire and fire people, that's so much power. Too much power for me, I'd be way too irresponsible with it: fire people on a whim, hire people to impress girls. I don't know how you resist the urge.
- Sometimes I'm like 'is he right?' and then I remember how long you've been doing this. I'll literally never have that much experience. You'll have to stuff my corpse and put it in my cubicle to even get close.

Notice in each instance I try to see things from his perspective, then I make a joke at my expense based on relative self-deprecation. It takes that extra step of re-framing your thought through their context and showing them that you empathize.

Customers

Joking with customers is fun, but you should keep in mind both the context of the job and the context of the customer. What I mean by that is that you don't want to say anything that would be shocking to either the company or the customer at all uncomfortable.

The rule of thumb that I use is to follow the customer's lead up until you hit the company's limit. Basically, if the customer doesn't joke, you don't joke. If the customer jokes, joke with them, but let them set the pace of content. You don't want to introduce topics, only accentuate them. If a customer is joking about the weather, you can joke about the weather. You don't know anything about the customer, so you don't want to introduce context. You want to let them be your guide for tone and content.

By company limit, I mean the tone and content you know to be acceptable within your company. If the customer starts talking about doing crystal meth and beating up hookers, and you work at Chuck-E-Cheese, you probably shouldn't follow his lead on content. Follow your customer's lead to your company's limit, after that there's no benefit to joking anymore. Also, if you want a customer to laugh at your jokes, laugh at theirs. The more it feels like a back and forth, the more the customer will get involved. It's a partnership, not a competition.

The trick to being funny at work is to tone down your edge by saying the same thing in a slightly more SFW fashion. The bar for what is funny at work is much lower than in public since everyone is a work version of themselves. You want to avoid constant negativity, and work on jokes that are hidden compliments. By being a positive but funny energy in the office, you can make yourself indispensable. And by injecting even a touch of humor in your cover letter and interview, you can stand out from the pack as someone who is both clever and pleasant to work with.

Chapter 9 – Funny for Friends

Nobody likes to admit it, but making friends as an adult is a strangely difficult task. As someone who's moved cities countless times, I know how difficult it is to find people to hang out with. By the time you're a grown up you have so many responsibilities and commitments that adding a new friend is a big ask, so if you expect someone to add you into their life, you have to bring value. That value can be anything, but in the case of this book it's funny. If you're a person who is always fun to be around, people will want to be around you. It's that simple.

However, adults are also a lot more set in their ways and have deeply set opinions and values, so when you first meet someone, you have to be very wary of their context. They see the world the way they see it, and no flippant joke from a stranger is going to change that. So you want to try to be as cognizant as possible of their context, and pick up on what you can right away. As the friendship evolves you can start to impose more of your particular sense of humor on them, but at the start you want to be as flexible and empathetic as possible.

Making friends and keeping friends are two very different tactics, so let's look at them separately.

9.1 Making Friends

The first step in winning friends over with your humor has absolutely nothing to do with being funny at all. It's the first step towards winning friends by any method, and it's the biggest hurdle a lot of adults have in the whole process. And that is putting yourself in a position to meet people. I've seen so many adults sit at home and do nothing and wonder why they don't have friends. Without school there isn't a reliable way to meet a steady stream of new people, so you have to do the legwork yourself. Join a sports league, join a club, volunteer, go to AA if you must, but put yourself in places where you're forced to interact with strangers. And they're forced to interact with you. It doesn't matter how funny you are, if you no one talks to you you'll never impress anyone.

Be sure that the activity you choose has regular meetups because adults take a couple of forced hangouts before they can become friends. By this age we're all very wary of someone who is too eager to spend time with us, we assume they're up to something. So, what you want to do is simply be a funny, engaging person for the first few forced hangouts, and draw people into you. You want the friendship to happen organically so that people who really mesh with you are the ones you're spending time with. You want to make it, so people start to get excited to see you, and then when you suggest meetings outside of the structured event they are elated. The trick to making friends is being the kind of person people want to be friends with. The truth is that most adults are starved for friendship but too stuck in their ways to make friends. Make them want to make an exception for you. Also, most adult meetings are focused around being social. The adult basketball league I'm in isn't about getting better at basketball, we're all too old and fat for that. It's about hanging out and meeting people. If you can be a beacon of fun during these meetings, you'll find yourself with a wealth of friends.

With that said, let's get to the practical tips.

Be Engaging

The most important thing to do when being funny to strangers is simply paying attention to people who are talking. The benefit of this is twofold. First of all, it helps you understand the context of the person you're speaking with. Actively listening to them helps you ascertain their point of view, beliefs, and experience.

This helps you craft funny moments that fit this person exactly. Beyond that, if you're clearing listening and taking in what someone is saying, that act alone draws them toward you. We all fear that no one is listening when we are talking, so if someone is speaking and they look over and see you giving them your full attention, it feels great. They remember that. And if you take that further and fully engage with them - I mean laugh at their jokes, add tags to what they say, ask interesting questions – they will start to seek you out. We all remember the people who laughed at our jokes when no one else did – be that person!

It's such a small thing, but by simply being the person who pays attention when no one else does, you become incredibly likable. I know a lot of us have the image of a cool, aloof, funny person in our heads, but in everyday life that person is alone. The true person who is remembered as a funny person is the one who makes you feel special. The one who makes you feel funny too. It's the easiest thing in the world to do and it is unbelievably powerful when it comes to making friends.

Mull it over
Engage with confidence

I wasn't lucky enough to be born with natural charm. Any ounce of charisma in me is stolen from people I've studied. And one thing I've found is that truly charismatic people leave others with the same impression:

They made me feel like I was the most important person in the room.

If you want people to like you, give them that feeling. Make them feel special. Ask them about themselves. Make eye contact. Listen. Treat what they say as interesting and important. Make jokes, but about the things they're talking about. Don't make fun of them, make them fun.

And most vitally...

Do not make everything about you. When they talk, don't relate it to you. Keep it about them. Make jokes with them about what they're talking about. If you're having fun listening to them, they'll have fun talking. This not only makes them more likely to find you funny, it makes them more likely to like you.

Be Patient

One of the main mistakes people make when trying to be funny is that they force it too often. This is doubly true when first meeting someone. Forcing a bad joke at a time when it's not natural is way more of a negative than a good joke is a positive. You want your first stab at a joke to be a real winner. If you've been unfunny a couple of times before hitting anything good, this stranger is going to think of you as annoying. You want to make sure that your first attempt has the best possible chance of making this person laugh. Before you even take a cut, listen for a while. Learn about the person. Wait for just the right opportunity and make your first impression a homerun.

Self Deprecate

One of the quickest ways to endear yourself to a group of strangers is to make fun of yourself. Everyone likes to laugh but every joke has a victim, and in a group of strangers where no one is aware of anyone else's context, picking a victim is risky. It's way too easy to stumble upon a subject that is sensitive for some of your audience. The easiest solution is to pick yourself. If you make fun of yourself (properly) it gives those strangers permission to laugh without hurting anyone's feelings. It's infinitely more likeable than making fun of another stranger, and if it's done properly, it actually projects confidence as opposed to weakness. The trick is to do it right.

I've mentioned it before, but the secret to successful self deprecation is that the audience must think that you're not actually bothered by the subject matter. If you make fun of yourself for being fat but, you're really sad and insecure about your weight, that's going to come across. The real power of self deprecation is when it's used to take power over the things that we're insecure about. And that only works if you can reign in your insecurity.

A very simple way to avoid it is to make fun of something that you're doing as opposed to something you are. *I'm eating like a fat pig* is infinitely less pity inducing than *I'm such a fat pig.* By attacking an action instead of an attribute, the overall tone is much softer and much more inviting for people to laugh at. In the case of being at an activity with strangers, I find the best way to weasel my way in is to be self depreciating about the activity we're doing. If I signed up to a bowling league to meet people, the first thing I would do is make fun of myself for everything bowling. Here are some examples:

- *I think these shoes have literally regrown my virginity*
- *I love bowling because it's the only professional sport I still have the body for*
- *I know it isn't the point, but I can guarantee that I'm better at gutterballs than anyone else here*
- *If you swapped my bowling scores with my golf scores I would look great at both*

I think you get the idea. All of the jokes are aimed at me, but none of them feel *sad*. They are all clearly lighthearted jabs at the current activity. You can expand this out for any activity, and these jabs at yourself are an excellent way to start conversations with strangers.

Aside from the current activity, another great time to employ self deprecation is when someone is talking about other activities they are into. Basically, if someone tells you they run marathons, it's a great time to tell them what a horrible runner you are. It's a solid technique because it both makes you look modest and makes them feel good about something of which they are proud. You have to do it the right way though, because if you do it improperly, you look like you're trying to hijack the conversation.

What you want to do is take a quick jab at yourself, and then throw it back to them with a question. That way it's obvious that you're not trying to dominate and that you are actually interested in what they are saying. Stick with the marathon example, let's go through some self depreciating jokes you could use.

Them: I like to run, I'm doing a marathon next month

- *That's amazing. I don't know how you do it. If you see me running, you better run with me because something awful is chasing me. How long have you been running?*
- *Oh wow, I get tired driving that long. Is it your first marathon?*
- *I'm planning on doing a marathon myself soon, I've been on the carbo loading stage for 10 years now. Any advice?*

Notice how in each case I take a really quick jab at myself, and then throw the ball back to them. This shows that I am actively listening enough to quickly form a thought about what they are saying, but also interested enough to want them to go on. You get a quick laugh and then throw back to them, and you can rinse and repeat as they speak. Just make sure to not overdo it and come off as obnoxious.

Train Your Brain
Make fun of yourself stupid

Self deprecation is an incredibly powerful tool for getting reactionary laughs, and the best part is that you can prepare in advance.

In this exercise, you have to find things about you *that you aren't sensitive about and* prepare jokes for them. Try to view yourself as other people see you, because the jokes don't work unless it's obvious to other people. Write as many jokes as you can.

Are you overly tall?
- *You know in college they called me the concert ruiner*

Are you overweight?
- *If we're ever on a boat and it sinks, stick near me. I'm buoyant as shit.*

Do you talk too much?
- *I know it's very out of character, but I have something to say about this!*

Are you a bit clumsy?
- *I've got all the dexterity of detoxing heroin addict.*

Pick the traits you want to make fun of and prepare jokes for as many situations as you can think of.

Live for little moments

You want to keep your eye out for those little moments that happen to each of us every day that make us go *huh, that was weird.* A squirrel won't stop staring at you, the elevator button won't work at first, some bird shit just misses you: innocent but odd things that happen all the time. They're not big things, but they make you pause and notice. Normally they're moments just for us because we're the only ones who see them and they're not quite important enough to tell people about. But if you can notice them happening to other people, you can make them feel as though you understand them.

Whenever something weird happens to us or around us, the first thing we instinctually do is look around to see if anyone else noticed it. If someone did, we immediately have that unique **shared context.** Hopefully by this point I've made it clear how important this can be. It immediately means that you and this person have something unique to just the two of you, and that is very powerful. Any joke you add on top of that only helps solidify that.

Mind you, don't watch people like a hawk and be there for every single moment. But if you see something odd happen to someone, make eye contact with them as a sign of acknowledgement, and if you can think of an appropriate joke, go for it. For example, if someone just barely misses getting shit on by a bird, wait for them to make eye contact with you and then say something like:

> *They say it's good luck to get shit on by a bird, but I'd say being just missed is much luckier.*

The joke doesn't have to be strong because the tension of the moment is big. You just want to release that tension and give both of you permission to laugh. You'd be amazed at how far this little technique can go to winning over strangers and making friends.

Gentle Ribbing

One of the best parts about having close friends is the fact that you can make fun of each other relentlessly and no one gets hurt. That isn't the case when you're making friends. When you first meet people, you want to treat them with kid gloves so that you don't offend. That doesn't mean you can't poke at them lightly, but you want to err on the side of not hurting anyone's feelings. In fact, before you ever start making fun of strangers, I suggest you take a couple of shots at yourself first. You want the audience to know that your jokes aren't mean spirited, and you wouldn't say anything to them that you wouldn't say to yourself. This is the best way to ensure that no one is taking your jokes to heart.

Once you have it established that you are a joker and your insults are toothless, you can start to think about how you can tease strangers in such a way that they still like you. A good starting point is the same rule that we used for self deprecation: make fun of actions, not attributes. You don't ever want to make fun of something that is out of a stranger's control. Hell, it's bad form to make fun of things your friends can't control unless you're absolutely certain that it's not going to offend them. It's easy to think that it's just for fun and it's not personal, but you never know what someone's sore spots are. By keeping to actions and not attributes we are making fun of what someone is doing, not what someone is.

But you have to be careful to ensure that you're picking the right actions. If you want to make friends, don't make fun of someone for earnestly trying to do something. If someone is bad at bowling, don't make fun of them for that. Your friends? Sure. But strangers could be sensitive to that kind of thing, especially coming from an unknown source. You want to instead look for things that mean nothing. Little slips. Someone misses their straw when try to take a drink, they call something by the wrong name, they lose their train of thought and trail off. Things that won't be embarrassing when brought up. These are what you want to focus on.

In these situations, the intent and tone of the joke make all the differences in the world. The overall goal of your joke is to say: *we've all been there.* As opposed to an attacking tone which would be more like *look at this idiot.* You are trying to create a sense of understanding and sympathy as opposed to humiliation. This creates more of a welcoming inclusive feel that makes people want to be around you. For example, if your friend spills some ketchup on their shirt, an attacking tone would be something like this:

> *I don't know if anyone's told you, but you're actually supposed to put that in your mouth and not on your chest.*

It's a funny joke, but it shames the person. If you want to make the person like you, you could try something more like this:

> *I feel you, I've got a whole drawer full of shirts with that exact same stain on them. I keep them 'cause they match with my mustard stained pants.*

See how the tone is sympathetic as opposed to accusatory? It just takes the extra second of thinking about your tone to change something from pushing people away to drawing them towards you.

You want to start with this extra gentle position, and as you get to understand people's context and their humor, you can start to push it a little more. Some people absolutely love being teased, and some people hate it. By starting at the safest position and slowly working your way forward you can make sure to draw as many people as possible towards you.

Storytelling

Telling stories to people is a great way to give them a little window into your life and let them know a bit about your personality. By doing it the right way, you can make yourself seem like someone that people want to hang out with. You want to tell engaging, funny stories that draw people into you. Of course, all of the same guidelines from our earlier chapter on storytelling apply here, but there are some extra things you should keep in mind when telling stories with the purpose of making people like you.

- **Keep it short**: we're all sceptical of strangers, so keep your stories as short as humanly possible. I mean shorter than whatever you're thinking right now. Ideally almost to the point of setup, punchline. You don't want these people waiting because they will get uninterested. Get right to the point.

- **Keep it contextless**: One of the great things about doing stand up is that every night you're presented with a room full of strangers, so you inherently learn how to tell stories that require no background information. Since these people are strangers, you want to do the same thing. You have to imagine hearing you're hearing the story without knowing anything about yourself. It has to make sense *and* be funny without relying on the person's opinion of anything, including yourself.

  That goes double for character traits about yourself. Too often I hear friends of mine tell stories that are only funny if the listener knows the storyteller intimately. A lot of people tell stories about things that happen to them that are only funny if you know details about the person. Like they'll tell a story about a horrible date they went on where they got taken to a Chinese restaurant, *can you believe that??* And if you didn't know that they were deathly allergic to MSG, the story would mean nothing.

It's difficult to get your head around sometimes, but it's incredibly important if you want to tell stories to strangers properly.

- **Leave out names unless they add to it:** These people don't know you, they might not ever know you. If you aunt fell over the couch and her dress flew up and now you can't unsee the horror, we don't need to know your aunt's name to appreciate the story. Keep out details like names and ages that are important when speaking to friends, but just get in the way talking to strangers. Extra information distracts from the humor of the story, not add to it. Don't add names unless they add to the story.

- **Discuss your current situation:** These people don't know much about you except for whatever is going on currently, so that is the only context that you have to work with. While stories are good at showing strangers other parts of your life, if you can tie it into whatever the current setting is, it makes strangers pay more attention. What I'm trying to say is lie. Whatever story you want to tell, make it fit the current situation. Pretend your story happened on the way to the meeting, or while you were preparing, or some sort of hook to draw in the listener. The more you can exploit that shared context the more successful you're going to be.

- **Be relatable:** Talk about situations that people are going to empathize with. I hate the term *check your privilege*, but unless you want people to think you're a douche, it's something you have to do. A lot of times our stories are complaints about things that happened to us, which is fine, but you have to ensure that you're reading the room. If you're complaining about money, you best be as broke or broker than your audience. If you're telling a story about a bad dating experience, it better be as bad or worse than your audience. There's nothing that turns people off quicker than someone complaining about a problem that you'd love to have. *You wouldn't believe it, I crashed my BMW into my Audi and now I'm driving around in my son's Honda like a commoner* might be a funny story at some upper crust black tie gala, but at a volunteer soup kitchen, you're an asshole.

If you keep these few things in mind, you can start to craft stories to tell strangers. Keeping it tied to the current event means that you'll always have an opening to tell it. As always, pay attention to your audience and make sure that they're enjoying what you're saying. If they aren't, pack up and move on. You're not going to win over people who don't like you by telling stories, so don't double down on this technique as a lifeline. You want to start with the shorter form jokes above, and as people start to warm to you, move deeper into stories. The more cache you have with your audience, the longer your stories can be. But at the start, short short short. This is what happened; this is my funny take on it. Get your point across, get your laughs, and then let someone else have a turn. Be engaging with them, listen, laugh, and then pick your spots.

By mastering these techniques you'll start to get more and more comfortable talking to strangers. I've moved cities many times, and every time I do I join a basketball league. Within two or three weeks I have a group of friends who do more than play basketball; we hang out all the time. You can do the same. Make sure you're seeing this people regularly, be funny and engaging so that they are enjoying their time too, and then make the jump from forced hangout to friends. It's often as easy as asking if they want to go for a drink or coffee after the hangout. If they're having a good laugh with you, chances are they will.

Train Your Brain
Write stories for strangers

Telling contextless stories to strangers is difficult and intimidating, but the only way to get better is practice. This exercise is for exactly that:

1. Think of a short, easy story. For this instance, let's use something that happened to you. Maybe you got shit on by a bird, maybe you spilled a whole pot of soup on yourself before a date, maybe you called your boss Mom.
2. Imagine telling this to someone with no knowledge of you or your life. Remove references, remove backstory, leave just the facts.
3. Put it in the funniest format you can (setup jokes, punch at the end).
4. Regardless of when the incident happened, write the story as though it just happened (urgency helps the audience appreciate the story)
5. Tell it to yourself over and over again to get it right and to make sure someone with **no context** would understand why it is funny.
6. Get into a conversation with a stranger (cab driver, plane seatmate, friendly cashier)
7. Tell them the story. If they didn't laugh, rewrite and try again.

The only way to get good is to be bad at first. Keep trying until you get a bulletproof contextless story!

9.2 Keeping Friends

As hard as meeting new friends as an adult is, it can be even more difficult to maintain that friendship. You've both got fully developed lives, and cutting out a significant chunk of time for a new friend can be tricky. You have to really want to hang out with them. I've had dozens of potentially great friendships wilt on the vine for a variety of different reasons. Some were unavoidable, but if I'm honest, a lot were my fault.

There have been times where I've gone too aggressive with jokes and hurt people's feelings. There have been times where my humor just doesn't click with the other persons, and we can't get a rhythm. And sometimes I've just been flat out boring. These are all things I can avoid if I had put in a little more effort.

We must be careful with our friends, especially new friends, because while we feel like we know them and their sense of humor, a lot of the time we're wrong. We form a picture of that person in our head, and we think we know them inside and out, but if we don't pay attention to their responses objectively, we can end up pushing them away.

It's not a fun trick or an easy answer, but the truth is that empathy is the root of both humor and friendship. The better you can understand their point of view, their context, the better you can give them what they need. It's easy to lose sight of this when you're joking in a group, and teasing can quickly turn into bullying. You might not notice because it feels like everyone is laughing, but crossing that line from playful to hurtful is a really easy way to lose friends. In the meantime, teasing done right is a great way to build closeness in a friendship and is the main way that funny people have fun in groups.

Striking that balance of aggressive enough to get laughs, but playful enough to not be hurtful is how you master the art of being a funny friend.

Busting Balls

Busting Balls is a stupidly outdated term that comedians (and others) use to describe friends making fun of each other. With comedians, this can be downright brutal. My best friends have said things to me that you wouldn't say to your worst enemy. You don't want to go that far, but you want to be able to playfully make fun of your friends and encourage them to do the same to you.

The first place to start is something we covered in the making friends section: make fun of yourself first and often. This reminds everyone that your jabs are not serious, and anything you'd say about them you'd gladly say about yourself. Hand-in-hand with this is laughing at yourself when other people tease you. You must be able to take any joke in order to be able to give any joke. Encourage the laughter and add to it, and that opens them up to laugh at themselves when you make fun.

In the same vein, if someone doesn't enjoy being made fun, don't make fun of them. It's uncomfortable for other people and it makes them secretly hate your guts. Try to stick to targets who enjoy the back and forth and can laugh at themselves. And even when you do have people who enjoy the game, be careful not to pile one. Sometimes everyone in the group will gang up on one person, and it can become too much. Remember empathy and do mental checks to make sure everyone is still having a good time.

Picking the things to make fun of is arguably the most difficult part. Again, the safest thing to do is to stick with actions instead of attributes. But with friends you can extend it a little further and make fun of attributes that *the friend makes fun of first.* I'm balding, and I make fun of it all the time, which opens it up for my friends to make fun of as well. They tell me when we're walking through a crowd, they follow my bald spot like it's the North Star. They know it's ok to do that because I've introduced the topic to the group. Sticking to these rules will ensure that you're not bringing up sensitive topics.

The other rule that you absolutely have to stick to is that the joke has to be substantially funnier than it is mean. Way too often I see people try to be playful but their saying mean things to their friends faces. The way to make sure of this is to avoid simply pointing out the dumb thing that your friend did or said, and instead add an actual joke. If your friend is speaking and their voice cracks, don't just say *ha your voice cracked you're stupid.* Or even *what are you 12?* Instead try to add another layer to it. The obvious joke is that the person is going through puberty, but instead of saying it, imply it. Say something like *Aw, this is a very exciting time for you! You're going to start noticing a lot of changes to your body, but it's perfectly normal.* You're using irony to imply that he's going through puberty, but that extra layer changes it from an insult to an obvious joke. The more you obscure the insult by adding layers, the less insulting you are. And also, the cleverer you look.

Timing is also important in keeping a joke funny instead of mean. Don't be too eager. You don't want to jump in the second one of your friends' goofs up. It's a real quick way to look like an asshole. You come off as the kind of dick who is sitting there waiting for your friends to mess up so you can jump down their throats. You never want to interrupt someone to insult them. It's much more effective to wait until they've finished their sentence and word your joke to work then. If by the time they've finished talking it's been too long since the slip up, you should just let it go. This keeps you from being the person to catch every single slip up as well, because that person is a dick too.

All those rules in place, here are some practical examples of good friend-building burns formats you can use:

- **Clothing**: It's pretty easy to tease your friends when they're wearing something that varies wildly from their usual attire. If they're dressed slightly better than normal you can ironically ask them what fancy activity they have planned (*Where are you going, prom?*). If they're dressed worse than usual (not for a sad reason) you use the same kind of ironic questioning (*Did you rob a homeless guy on the way here?*). The laughs come from pointing out the difference, so as long as you add a layer to it, you can make fun of anything.

New hat: *Jesus, how bad was the haircut?*
Sweat pants: *Someone give you a gift certificate to Depression 'R' Us?*

Whatever it is, pick it out, add a layer, and take a shot.

As always, be empathetic. Don't attack people's clothing if you think it's going to upset or humiliate them. If you're worried you might be close to doing so, follow up your joke with an earnest compliment or apology complete with self deprecation. Taking a shot at yourself will instantly soften the shot you just took at someone else. *I'm just jealous because I tried to wear that hat and looked like a douche, but you're actually pulling it off.*

These are your friends, and the intent should never be to hurt. Make sure they always know you're only joking, and try to balance out your sarcastic comments with reassurances of your friendship. It's only fun if everyone is having fun.

- **Activities:** If you can see your friends doing something out of character, simply pointing it out is enough because you've caught them mid-action, and the realization of what they're doing and that you've noticed is usually enough. Plus you normally won't have time to think up a joke before they're done. But what happens more often is that you'll hear someone talk about something they've done out of character.

Like for instance I recently started running, which is not something I would have done in the past. When I told my friends I tried running, the first thing they said was: *I assume running is a new restaurant that opened downtown.* Great joke, hurt a bit but made me laugh a lot. That format works great – pretending to be so shocked that the very word must mean something different.

Again, you're looking for actions that are out of place. So something you wouldn't have expected them to be doing. All you have to do is spot the action, craft your joke, and you're golden.

- **Likes:** A secret about people is that everyone is inconsistent. People are complex, and as much as you think you can pigeonhole someone, they will almost always surprise you. You may think a metalhead would be hardcore in all their tastes, but I guarantee they have a soft spot for a Britney Spears song or a Sisterhood of the Travelling Pants style movie. The trick is to learn how to dig for it.

Asking your friends directly if they like things, or what their favourite whatever is can be a great way to drill down to find funny and interesting things about your friends. For an example, I have the palette of a 10-year-old, and all my friends know it. A fun game that they like to play that always ends in laughter is that anytime they think of an obscure food they ask me if I like it. Normally I either don't like it or haven't tried it – which gives them a chance to rehash old jokes about how awful my diet is, a topic we all enjoy – but on the rare occasion where I *do* like it, the laughter is even louder. *How can you like black liquorice when you don't even like pasta??* And they all howl.

Basically, you want to ask them if they like something that would be out of character for them. Because then if they don't it you can tease them about what they do like. This is usually non-offensive because it's reinforcing their image. I'm comfortable having a terrible diet so it's fine to make of it. And if they do like the thing, everyone gets to have a good laugh at the surprise.

There are also lots of organic ways that these likes can come up, and their even better. The skill is in being able to understand how people are perceived, that way you know when things are out of character. It has to be obvious enough that the audience also recognizes it as out of character, and also not be something that might humiliate the person. But all in all, it's a very non-attacking way to joke around with your friends.

These are just some examples, but the idea is that you don't ever want to be attacking who your friends are. You want to make sure you're only ever making fun of inconsequential things, and that you are mixing in self deprecation and earnest statements so that your friends know that you actually care about them and you're making fun in the purest sense: you want everyone to have fun.

Mull it over
Make sure the balls don't actually bust

There's nothing I love more than back and forth insults with my friends. We love cutting each other up, and in general nothing is off limits. That said, there have been many times that one of us have gone too far and hurt feelings. Here are some things to keep an eye out for to ensure everyone is having fun:

1. **Avoid piling on:** if it feels like one person is taking a sustained beating, back off. If everyone is picking on the same person, that person is going to get hurt.
2. **Fire back:** if there is a hard shot at someone, take the next shot at whoever sent it. By keeping the target moving you avoid any one person taking too much
3. **Gauge reactions:** if the person your teasing isn't teasing back, apologize and move on. It's only fun if they're fighting back
4. **Keep Secrets Secret:** only pick on things that everyone knows about. You should never reveal a fact in a joke, the fact needs to be common knowledge.
5. **Avoid hot buttons:** if someone is self conscious about something, consider it off limits. Make fun on inconsequential things, not real triggers.
6. **Shoot yourself too:** if you think you might be going too hard, take some shots at yourself. Show them that it's all just in fun.

Comebacks

Part of friends teasing each other is knowing how to take a joke and fire back with a zinger of your own. It's not an easy task because time is short, and pressure is high. But with the right approach you can give yourself the best opportunity to succeed. Here's the process I go through when I find myself in that situation.

1. Examine the context of the insult coming my way. Is it about my appearance? About something I did? About something I said? The context of the incoming joke needs to be a part of the outgoing joke. You can't just fire back with a random unrelated insult.

    Did you steal that jacket from Liberace's coffin?
    Well you're a fat fuck!

    That's not being clever, that's just being an asshole. You want to fire back with an actual joke, and since there's no setup you need to use the previous jokes context.

2. Check the jokes context against the context of the person who insulted you. There's a chance they're oblivious to the fact that they're guilty of a similar offense. If someone makes fun of your jacket while they're wearing a lime green fedora, you can insult that back. Remember, that the easiest insult to craft quickly is often of the *you look variety.* So you could hit back with something like *I'm not taking fashion advice from someone who dressed like a failed magician.* If they point out something off about you and you can point out something equally off about them, you'll be the one with the bigger laugh. This goes for anything from physical objects to actions to personality traits. When someone jokes about you, check to see if

you can throw it right back at them.

For the love of God don't use the exact same thing they use unless it's unbelievably apparent how bad theirs is. If they jokingly call you stupid and you respond with *yeah well you're stupid*, you really are the one who looks stupid. If you can't find any similar dirt on them, it's alright, just move on to the next step.

3. If you can't find a suitable flaw in the other person, you can try to go the other way and lean into the flaw and point out that *despite* that flaw, you're still superior, and off the back of that create an insult. It sounds complicated, but it's the actually pretty simple. Here's an example: I've got a friend with upsettingly nice hair, and he likes to make fun of my balding. When he does, I like to fire back with some variation of *and yet somehow women still like me more than you. What's that say about your personality?*

    You're accepting the context, and then using a relative boast to shift the context to something you can create an insult about. It's a little more complicated than the last step, but it lets you make an unrelated insult seem related. It's a beautiful little technique that is really impressive to the audience. Turn the flaw into a relative boast, then turning that boast into an insult. Here's another example using the jacket insult from above:

    Did you steal that jacket from Liberace's coffin?
    Yeah, I needed something to make me look ridiculous. Of course you don't need any help since you've got that face.

You accept the insult, turn it into a relative boast (I'm less ridiculous looking than you), and then insult off the back of that.

If you can't think of anything suitable immediately, move on to step 4.

4. If you can't find a good insult comeback or don't want to insult for whatever reason, you can always double down on the insult and attack yourself. If you do it with dignity it's a great way to keep the laughs going.

    Did you steal that jacket from Liberace's coffin?
    Yeah, I was sick of looking only kind of stupid so I thought I'd really kick it up a notch.

    It's a nice, simple way to take back the upper hand, and no one gets hurt.

5. If you can't think of a good comeback but you still want to take the power back, a very good way to neutralize an attack is to agree with it in an almost bored tone. It's not going to get a lot of laughs if you use it all the time, but occasionally it can catch people off guard.

    Did you steal that jacket from Liberace's coffin?
    Yes.

    There's nothing really they can come back with after that, so it's the end of the run, but if you're real desperate for an out you can always use this.

Get a laugh right now
Be the Comeback Kid

Here are some premade comebacks you can have ready for someone making fun of you for various things.

Appearance:
- *Yeah but I'd take my face over your personality any day.*
- *I can put on makeup. Unfortunately there's no concealer for your disgusting soul*

Weight:
- *I can lose the weight way easier than you can lose the ugly*
- *You laugh but we'll see who lasts longer in the apocalypse. I could live for years off these fat stores*

Money
- *It says in the bible that it's easier for a camel to pass through the eye of a needle than for a rich man to get into heaven. It also says you're a douchebag*
- *You're lucky I'm poor, if I had money I'd never hang out with you losers*

Clothing
- *I thought it was a dumb shirt too but it made your mom so wet I couldn't throw it out*
- *I can't help it, I don't understand fashion. You know, like you with [women/men]*

Haircut
- *I told them to make me look like you*
- *I figured I'd ugly myself up to give you a chance to compete*

Preparing comebacks ahead of time can make you look

like a genius in the moment. Try to think ahead to all the things people might tease you for, and have as many comebacks ready as possible. You'd be surprised how often this comes in handy.

Keep it in the air

Making fun of each other is good fun, but the best way for a group to really get laughing is to attack an outside target. If everyone in the group can focus in and make fun of the same thing, they can produce a laugh like no other. The trick to getting the most laughter out of these situations is to get as many jokes out of the same topic as possible. Switching topics is risky and energy consuming, so when you get on a roll with a topic you want to try your best to keep it going as long as possible. There are two ways to do that and figuring out how to use both and switch between them is the key to rolling laughter.

- **Tags:** Whenever someone makes a joke about a topic you want to come up with as many relevant tags as the audience can enjoy. Remember that a tag is an extra punchline that doesn't require an additional setup. So if someone makes a joke about Trump's hair (*Have you seen his hair? I mean, you'd think it was a wig, but if you picked your hair you'd never pick that one*), you want to use that same setup to keep making that use that setup (*it looks like the dried out carcass of some deep sea animal – see how there is no additional setup?*) for as long as people keep laughing. There are legit diminishing returns here, so don't try to force them whne the laughs die. Think of it like microwave popcorn – when the laughter starts to become sparse, pull the plug. It's not going to start back up again using that same setup, that's one of the unwritten rules of comedy

- **Fresh Angles:** When a premise naturally dies out, the only way to keep the laughs moving is to find a new but related angle on the same premise. So for instance, when the laughs about Trump's hair die out, the only way to restart them is to create a new setup that is related to the last one. That connection is important, because it allows you to carry over the humor from the previous joke to this one. So, when we're done tagging Trump hair jokes, I need to find a new, but related Trump angle. Assuming we had a good laugh at the hair and I want to keep it moving, I could say something like this:

The hair is so bad that sometimes it makes me forget that he's got the skin color of a jaundiced oompa-loompa.

See how I've related it to the last joke, but I've created a whole new setup and joke. It allows us to carry over the goodwill from before, but move it to a new setup. Then we can all bat this setup around until the tags run out and we can repeat the process again.

Note that there are also diminishing returns on new angles, so again, when the laughter is dead, it's time to move to a new premise. That said, if you can manage to find a completely unique and clever angle it is possible to resuscitate a topic briefly, but it will die out quick after that. Pay attention to your audience and don't force extra tags and angles that people don't appreciate.

- **Rebirth:** When you're done laughing at your friend's idea, feel free to bring it back up after a little bit of time. Even though it may have died out, if it was a real winner everyone will appreciate revisiting it 20 minutes later. Bring it back to life by repeating one of the best lines. It will get everyone laughing again.

Telling Stories

Storytelling in some form is often a sort of the backbone of new funny ideas for friend groups. Generally, when something even kind of funny happens to funny people, they can't wait to tell their friends. They know that everyone will have a good laugh, but also that the input from other friends will only make the experience funnier. You know that they'll ask funny questions and have funny insights. Continually bringing these kinds of moments to your friends is part of being funny.

We've gone over storytelling in detail so I won't repeat myself here, but I will add a couple of nuances that arise when telling stories to established friends.

- **Targeting:** you know your friends well, so you know what friends will appreciate what details of a story. Oftentimes, there will be a detail that will only be interesting to one or two members of the group, and not everyone. In these cases, conspicuously direct those parts at the people who will appreciate it. I mean right down to *Steve, you'll like this...* This does a couple of things. First of all, it ensures that the only party who is going to care is listening, which keeps you from getting nothing back on your story. You want to make sure the interested party is paying attention. But also, it lets the rest of the audience know that *you know* they're not necessarily going to get this part. It's small, but it changes the audience's mentality. If you don't call out who this part is directed at than the rest of the audiences is inclined to think you don't know what they'd like. Again, it's a little thing but over time it adds to people either thinking of you as funny or not.

- **Take chances:** These are already your friends, so more than likely they're going to have a little more patience for your stories than strangers would. This makes them a great place to try out stories for the first time. Remember that when you're telling a story you've got to rehearse and plan it out, but regardless of how much you plan ahead, you're not going to know how funny your story is until you tell it. Let your friends be your test audience and follow their reaction. With practice you'll find that you're able to make more and more mundane occurrences funny, but you can never do that without practicing.

- **Accept Ideas:** Listen to the tags and angles that your friends add to your stories. If you can start to surround yourself with funny people, you'll quickly notice that any story you bring to them gets even funnier with their input. Don't be afraid to hang on to their ideas and incorporate them into the story for when you tell others. I've said many times to not get too caught up in the truth, and because of that a story is never truly finished. There are always funny details you can add. Let your friends help you be the funniest storyteller you can be.

- **Learn to bomb gracefully:** It's ok if a story bombs with your friends, take it as a learning experience and not a personal slight. If you're telling a story that you think is hilarious but you're getting nothing from your friends, don't be a sook about it. Take a moment to check the current context of both your friends and the situation. Perhaps there are external reasons that they aren't laughing. If not, chances are very good that you're not explaining it properly. If you're sure it's funny, it's probably funny, but either you're not giving the proper context or the delivery is wrong. Both of those are correctable, but you have to accept that the problem is with your story and not your friends. You have to have the humility to deconstruct your story and rebuild it from the ground up so that you can get your message across. Your friends aren't just there to show you how great you are, they are also there to let you know when you're off base.

- **Learn from others:** If you have a friend who is a really good storyteller, pay attention and try to see what you can take from it. Is their wording interesting? Are they adding details specifically for laughs? How quick and often are their punchlines? There's nothing wrong with being influenced by other people, it's often the best way to learn these techniques. Cherry pick skills and phrasings and interesting words from stories that you particularly enjoy and try to meld them with your own style to form something unique. No one is a perfect storyteller, so be humble enough to pick up new skills where you can.

  At the same time, also pay attention to the bad storytellers. When someone is telling you a story that is horribly uninteresting, ask yourself why? What mistakes are they making that I too could be guilty of? Are they adding unnecessary details? Are they missing backstory? Are they assuming we know or feel things we don't? Finding things to avoid is just as important as finding things to copy when it comes to being the best storyteller you can be.

Overall, joking with friends can be the single most rewarding and fun activity you can imagine. My favourite nights are sitting around with a few of my funniest friends and laughing about everything. In fact, the goal of almost every conversation we have is to find a laugh. And if you can approach topics that way, it makes everything more fun. You want to surround yourself with people who have the same approach and learn from them. It's perfectly ok to pick up habits and tendencies of funny people, and they will do the same to you. As a group you can grow your humor by leaps and bounds by joking in a group. By using the techniques I've described in the making friends section, you will find yourself naturally gravitating towards funny people and having them gravitate towards you. Before long you can build a funny and reliable circle that will make any event a fun one.

The one warning I have to give you about being constantly surrounded by a funny group though is that it becomes more and more difficult to discern what is only funny because of shared context and what is objectively funny. Something I've seen countless times is people taking jokes that have evolved within their friend group and trying to export that to another group. And that simply doesn't work. The things that your group have batted around for minutes or days or weeks require that kind of background to appreciate. If you try to take the end product of a joke that has grown and mutated amongst your circle to someone else, they simply aren't going to appreciate it. It's changed too much from the original idea, and it requires someone to have come on that journey to get it. Keep your inside jokes on the inside, and try to build new ones from the ground up with new people. Otherwise, you come across as arrogant and grossly unfunny as you laugh your face off at something nobody else gets at all.

That warning aside, enjoy the gift of laughter with your friends and know that the group that jokes together stays together.

Chapter 10 – Love is Funny

It's no secret that women love funny men. It's often stated that the number one thing that women are looking for in a man is a sense of humor. It works the other way too, studies have shown that "in the long run, funny women satisfy men more" (medicalexpress.com). However, I'll be up front when I say that from the funny women that I know, it's not as straight forward to win a man over with humor. A lot of men are intimidated by women who are funnier than them. If that's you, stop. Dating a funny woman is a fantastic gift that only serves to up your funny game, so grow the hell up.

Regardless, it's pretty undeniable that a good sense of humor will help you in your dating game. A quick wit can help you flirt like you wouldn't believe, and learning the secret to complimentary jokes can help you butter someone up without being obvious. The ability to craft good jokes and stories makes the other person think of you as smart and warm, and it makes you infinitely more likeable and relatable. I'm telling you this as a reasonably ugly man – if you can take someone out and make them laugh the whole time, they'll want to see you again. You do that consistently each and every time you hang out with someone, and your chances of a successful relationship are much higher.

Before you get to the successful relationship part you have to meet someone; a task that has paradoxically gotten both easier and harder to do with the advent of the internet. It's easier to get in touch with people, but because of that people seem more disposable. It's easy for them to decide they don't like you and move onto the next person. You need to make yourself instantly stand out, and being funny is a great way to do that. In this section we'll go through all stages of relationships, from dating app icebreakers to keeping the laughter going in a long-term relationship.
The best way to get people to like you romantically is to be super hot, but the second-best way is to be funny.

10.1 Online

Meeting Someone

There's nothing more exciting and scarier than meeting someone new. There's unlimited potential in it – this person could be your soulmate! (because of course there's one perfect person out there for you, makes logical sense...) But that doesn't mean you shouldn't try. Mostly people meet online now, but we'll also look at techniques that can help you meet people in person. We're not talking about pickup lines here; this isn't The Game. It's more just about managing the context of the conversation to allow your humor to draw people in. But since it's an online dominated world now, that's where we'll start.

Profile

A funny profile is a great way to attract like-minded people towards you, but you have to be careful because there is no tone and no context for your jokes aside from what is on your profile. Jokes about yourself are the easiest, since they can be both disarming and endearing. The same rules apply to self deprecation as before: make sure it doesn't feel sad. And as always, a good way to do that is to make fun of actions and not attributes.

Good targets are things like your job or your hometown, things that don't define you as a person. *I'm a contractor so while I do great work in the bedroom, don't be surprised if the time estimate is a bit off and the cost a lot higher than we agreed upon.* The jokes don't have to be the greatest, you just want to show that you have a good sense of humor. Make sure to skew as non-offensive as possible because nobody likes an edgy profile. Your friends might tell you it's hilarious but everyone else thinks you're a douche.

Puns on your name are also easy pickings. Also a funny (perhaps made up) fact about yourself that makes you seem interesting. Jokes about your pictures also work. The idea is to make fun of yourself in such a way that people don't read it and assume that you have low self esteem. Even if you do, try to hide it at least for your profile.

Don't get hung up in making the perfect joke, just get one good line in about yourself with some light self deprecation and that's enough to let people know that you're funny and easy to talk to. If you try to saturate your profile with laughs, you're going to end up look like you're trying too hard. You want to leave them wanting more. Pick your best one or two and save the rest for the conversations.

Train your brain
A profile in humility

Regardless of how much experience you have with humor, it's not always easy to tell if something is funny. And a dating profile is harder than most.

Here's a real easy exercise that will go a long way to improving your dating profile: **Ask people's opinions**

Before you put your profile up, find people you trust and ask their opinion. Demand they be brutally honest. Hell, if you don't have anyone like that, ask strangers on the internet. They have no problem being honest.

And most importantly: **listen to the feedback**

A lot of the time people will subconsciously write profiles that are only funny **with context**. It only works if people know things about you, and it's difficult to know that without asking people.

Be humble. If they tell you it doesn't work, believe them. The audience is always right.

Icebreakers

In the world of online dating, you're going to have to start up a lot of text conversations, there's just no way around that. It's not everyone's preferred method of conversation, but given the medium, it's the best we've got for now. And the first step towards impressing someone through text is having a funny opening line. You've probably seen some good examples on Twitter or Reddit, but if you're copying ideas from a popular source there's a good chance you're going to get called out. You want to be able to craft unique and interesting first messages that stand out from the other dozen the person is getting.

As with everything we've talked about so far, the key to this is context. The more information you have about the person, the better tailored an opening line you can construct. Obviously in the case of online dating the only context we have to go by is their profile. Sure, maybe you could creep them heavy and get more information from social media, but, ah, don't do that. If you're gut instinct is to do that you should probably sort yourself out. Whatever is in their profile should be enough to create something special.

First step is that you need to skip the most obvious joke. Like if you're going to make a pun on the person's name, it' better be grossly elaborate. If it isn't, I guarantee they've heard it a thousand times. Your goal is to find a joke that you *know* no one else has opened with. It takes a little extra time, but like we said in the cover letter section, if you take that extra time for each message, you'll have a much higher success rate. You could crank out 100 generic messages, but they won't be nearly as successful as 10 well thought out, unique messages (I mean, unless you're real hot. Then the 100 generics will do just fine).

Here are some examples for opening jokes

- **Puns:** Listen, I don't condone this, I think it's a bit forced and lame, but I'll concede there are a few advantages. A real good never before heard pun can be impressive, and make you seem clever and funny. But a real good never before heard pun is not super easy to come up with. Especially for someone who possibly gets dozens of messages a week. Chances are good that they've heard whatever masterpiece you drum up, and if so, you look like a real knob. That said, if you're a wordplay fan and you like opening with a pun, put in the extra effort to make it unexpected. If the woman's name is Hope and you open with *You're my only Hope* take your phone and bash it into your face repeatedly. In order to be unique and memorable, you have to try harder. Everyone is going to use *Hope* as a pun, so you need to find another way to use that word in a pun. I find it's easier to start with the phrase and build around it. I would find a phrase that I could insert the word Hope and then work backwards to find my pun. So I start going through rhymes for Hope, the more complex but well known the better: soap on a rope, rope-a-dope, slope of a line, isotope, Constantinople, Oprah Winfrey, etc. etc. Then for each I try to think of a way to use it as a pun that is complimentary and pick from my choices.

Here are a few:

- *Everyone knows the slope of a line is y=mx+b. But did you know that the Hope of a line is u=beautiful.*

- *Listen, I don't want to start a geography war, so you can call it Istanbul all you want, but to me, it'll always be ConstantinHopel*

These show a level of care about your message and a bit of inventiveness, both of which help you get replies. By figuring out the phrase first and working backwards you can create long elaborate puns that are no more funny than short puns, but they show that you've individualized your message and put thought into it. And you can guarantee that your message is unique and bound to stand out. The puns aren't always going to be easy, and you probably shouldn't force it if you can't find something good.

- **Funny Statement:** If you look closely enough at anyone's profile you can find something to make a joke about. However, you don't want that thing to be the butt of the joke. If it says they're originally from Alabama don't open with something like *Originally from Alabama, that's fun. I know we're not related, but I hope you'll give me a chance anyway.* You want your question to be about the piece of information, but the victim to be something different. Try something more like *I have a confession, I'm not from the states, at first I thought Alabama was a Harry Potter spell.* By making yourself the victim but pulling the subject from their profile you've created a joke that isn't insulting but is designed to entice a response.

You can do this with pretty much anything from someone's profile, from movies they like to activities to places they've been in their pictures. If you see someone in front of the Eiffel tower you can make a joke about Paris. *I find it weird that they call Paris the 'city of love', I always thought that would be Intercourse, Pennsylvania.* Never making fun of the information you've obtained, but by keeping it tangentially related to something from their profile you show that you've taken the time to think about them.

- **Funny Question:** In my opinion I think a funny question is a better opener than a funny statement, because it encourages a response and opens the floor for the person to respond with something funny. A funny statement can be a dead end and is substantially less engaging. The context for the question should be gleaned from the bio/pictures as that's the only information you have available.

The tone of the question is key, because it's very important to ensure there is no way it could be taken as an insult. If a woman says they like The Office in their bio (as many do), asking something like *Do that many women actually love The Office or is that like some secret code for something?* Can be insulting because it's a slight shot at a show the person loves, as well as a gross shot at women in general. You want to avoid any sort of attacking tone, and keep it sillier. *If I admit to you that I've never seen The Office would that be a deal breaker? Because if so, I've totally seen and love every episode.* You're being (slightly) challenging, which is good for flirting, but notice that you're not attacking anything. The tone is very innocent and sort of shows you're willing to do what it takes to get to know the person. Also, you're inviting them to talk about their favourite show, which is a topic people usually like to discuss. Feigning ignorance is a good way to get people talking to you, because people love to explain things they like.

You can apply this to basically any activity that they enjoy. If they're into sports, ask a funny sports question: *How come wearing skin tight stretchy pants that show off your ass is a no-no for jocks UNLESS they're playing football?*

Hiking: *Be honest with me, do you really like hiking, or are you just hoping that one day you'll find a dead body and be on the news?*

Board Games: *I love Settlers of Catan! What would you trade me for some wood?*

Travel: *ok what if I told you I could give you the ability to travel anywhere in the world whenever you want, but every second trip has to be a two week long stay in Bend, Oregon. Are you in?*

You want to let your creativity shine through and think of a question you know they haven't heard before. The techniques for the questions are very similar to how we've created jokes all up until this point. You can use everything we've learned; you just need to form it into a question. The punchline doesn't need to be quite as strong because phrasing it as a question inherently adds some surprise. Putting a person on the spot with something they didn't expect generates laughter. Take the time to really study the bio and actually think about what it says. Take that information mull it over in your head until you've got an interesting angle. Then form that into a question and you're on your way.

- **Personal Story:** This is the most wide open category and one in which you should probably feel the least beholden to the truth. Basically, the idea is to latch onto something from their profile and tell a short, funny story related to it in an attempt to draw them in. There are a few things to keep in mind when doing this:

- Don't make it all about you. If it feels like a bragging

story or like you're only writing it to entertain yourself it will come off bad. You want to keep the audience in mind because you're doing this for them. Don't be the hero in the story or the cool guy, it's obvious to the reader.

- Don't make it too long. Keep things short enough so you're not boring

- Do make it related to them. This story is to intrigue them, so the more it seems about/related to them the more they are going to be interested.

- Don't be a creep. I don't know how to put this any nicer. Some of you are creeps and unaware of it, so assume that you're creepy and try to remove and trace of it.

- Do end with a related question so it's clear you're engaging them and not just entertaining yourself.

With those rules in place, you can start making up (or telling a real) story. Good seeds are things like hometowns, jobs, likes... things that you can relate to or pretend to relate to. For instance if someone is from a particular city, you can tell a story about your experience in that city. *I went to Montreal once when I was 12. I watched a man get mugged and a prostitute pulled out her breasts right next to them. My mother screamed and we had to go back to the hotel. It was the greatest day of my life. Is that common? Is that why you moved?*

It's not a hilarious story but it's interesting and related enough to grab someone's attention, which is all you're looking to do with an opener. It's doubly easy for activities. If someone is into swimming: *I have PTSD from swimming. When I was 12 I dove off the diving board and my trunks fell off and an entire old lady aquafit class saw me naked and laughed at me. Someday will you take me swimming so I can learn it's not all trauma?*

I'm the butt of the joke, and I've asked an engaging question. This endears you to the reader and encourages them to respond to you. A story like this allows you to show some vulnerability and humility and lets them know you're ok to laugh at yourself. This technique lets you get across whatever you want while still being funny and not worrying about offending anyone. As with all self deprecation, watch that you're not making it too believably sad. You want to be the butt of the joke, but you need to be dignified.

- **Challenge:** This technique takes a little more subtlety than the previous methods, but when it's appropriate it can be incredibly powerful. The idea is to take an opinion from the person's profile and disagree with it, and use that initiate a conversation. The finesse is doing this in a way that isn't insulting to the other person, but is more playful and flirty. A trick to make it easier is that the less consequential the opinion you challenge, the less likely you are to offend the other person. A very black and white example is something like sports teams. It's not really *your* team, so most people can take a joke about it. But still, your approach makes the difference. For instance, if you see someone wearing the uniform of a team that is a perennial loser (like the Toronto Maple Leafs) you could open with a challenging statement to that. But something like *If you're dumb enough to cheer for the Leafs you might just be dumb enough to date me* is insulting. You're making fun of both the team and the person. Instead, something like *It's a good call to wear that Leafs jersey, it makes you seem very non-threatening. No one in a Leafs Jersey ever beats anyone* puts all of the insult onto the team. This way you're only challenging their like, and not themselves.

You can extrapolate this to any other sort of opinion. Entertainment is an easy one: *Post Malone is this century's Fred Durst, fight me.* Just make sure that you're challenging the opinion and not the person. *You don't look like the kind of douche who would like craft beer* is challenging to the person, whereas *I refuse to believe craft beer is better than regular beer. No way some bearded guy named Dave who works in IT makes better beer than a company who's made it for hundreds of years* challenges the idea that craft beer is good.

By challenging something that they feel strongly about you're enticing a response out of them, because they need to defend themselves. If you can do this in a funny way (and the person has a sense of humor) it is a fantastic way to start a confrontational flirty conversation.

- **Randomness:** This concept spits in the face of everything we've gone over so far, and I think it's the least consistent. But the idea is to open with a question or a statement that is so completely surprising that it's funny. I have to stress, this is incredibly inconsistent. What is 'randomly funny' varies wildly person to person, and there's no way to tell if you're idea will click with the other person. And if it doesn't, there's no coming back from that. If you throw something random at a person that you think is hilarious and they think is dumb as mud, they're not likely to ever take you seriously. But if quantity over quality is your thing, you can execute this technique without reading the person's profile.

Obviously, this category is unbelievably wide open. Both the topics and the techniques are essentially endless, but the idea is that you want to surprise the person into laughing, but intrigue them into responding.

It's hard to cover everything in a category this vague, so let me give you some examples of ideas that I have used.

- **Random Question:** You want it to be unexpected, but it has to be intriguing enough that they want to answer. *If you had to choose between being super ugly vampire with only one arm or a super hot werewolf with herpes, what would you choose?* There's no right or wrong here, you're just hoping to hit on something they find interesting.

- **Roleplay:** Pretend you're someone else for a weird opening. *I know this is going to sound crazy, but I'm a time traveller from 100 years in the future. 2020 is more than just a bad year, it's the start of the end of the world. It turns out the only way to save it is for us to date!* You can pretend to be anyone or anything since all you're doing is trying to surprise them with something they've never heard before.

- **Surprise Energy:** Sometimes you can surprise people with your energy more so than your words. *Alright, fine, we can get married, but I swear to god if you don't stop talking shit about my mother I will divorce you, kids be damned.* Your goal is to catch them off guard and be amused in the confusion. As with all of the random techniques, it really depends on the person if this will work or not.

The only way to discover which of these techniques will work for you is to try them out and see which ones mesh with your sense of humor. As with everything, you're only going to improve if you practice, so take your openers seriously. Don't rush them, sit and try to craft a good one before you move forward. If you put in the work and take feedback honestly, you'll notice a huge change in your response rate.

Text Conversation

Ok, now that you've established a connection with someone, the next steps usually involve having a few conversations across text. This tends to be where a lot of connections fizzle out, as it can be hard to establish a rapport through text. It's a difficult way to communicate really, as all tone and subtlety is lost from your words. Also a lot of context is stripped away, since you can't know what is going on around someone that you are texting with. Because of this you have to be extra careful with your words. We often say things in our head before we text them and we don't realize that they have to be read a certain way or with a certain emotion behind them in order to get our point across. And with that lost, the other person can easily take something the wrong way.

As you can imagine, this makes joking through text extra difficult. So before you make any joke, you have to pause and analyze the situation closely. Try to look at the conversation so far: Have I assumed any of the tone? Is there any chance the other person perceives this differently than me? Is entire context for this joke present, or are there things you'd have to know to get it? You (likely) know next to nothing about this person, so you don't' want to assume that they are looking at things the same as you. Try to stick to jokes that are, for lack of a better term, obviously jokes. The more you're asking from your audience, the more likely the joke will fail in text.

Also, the flow of a text conversation is a lot different than that of a regular conversation. 'Zingers' (snappy comebacks to something said) tend to not fly nearly as well because timing is such an important part of it. *That's what she said* has a much higher bar for being funny though text than it does through speech because there's an inherent delay in texting. If you ever read a Friend's script it seems a lot less snappy in black and white. So you have to be more self critical of your jokes if you want to have any success in this medium.

All that negativity aside, there are huge advantages to text conversations - mainly the lack of a time crunch. You have an extra second/minute/hour to think of just the right response. This gives you the time you need to really work on your wording and get it just right before you hit send. If you use that properly, you can be sure that you are delivering the best version of your joke, and if you do that, it will compensate for the lack of tone. Overall, the ideas for how to make jokes through text are the same as they were for creating openers, except now you want to build the context from the conversation instead of the profile. You want to listen to what they are saying, empathize as best you can so you can try to see it from their side, then if appropriate, create something funny from that. All of the aforementioned techniques are in play, though I'd really try to restrict my use of randomness. I can't stress how unbelievably difficult it is to make that consistently funny and if you think you're being hilarious with it, chances are you're being annoying.

Mull it Over
Every text is a draft

If you want to be funny via text, the first thing you need to realize is that your first effort is never your best effort.

When making a joke via text to someone your trying to get to know, **never** send it as soon as you type. I can guarantee that more often than not, you're not saying exactly what you mean. Very few of us can instantly put our thoughts into words like that.

After you write a text out, stop, take a pause. You need to wait long enough that your brain moves onto other thoughts. Then go back and read the text without having it hot on your mind. You'll often find that you didn't quite get your point across the way you might have intended.

Questions

By far the most important technique to keep in mind with a newly blossoming text conversation is to ask **interesting questions**. Unlike with our openers, we want to make the questions a little less jokey than before. The goal here isn't always to get a laugh, but to show that we're interested and attentive. Adding humor to that makes it much more palatable. If you try too hard to make the questions funny it comes off as narcissistic, as though you don't actually care about what their saying and you're just trying to make yourself laugh.

There's no easy trick to creating interesting questions except to take the time to really think about what the person is telling you. If they tell you they work at a hair salon, try to picture what that would be like. What intrigues you about a day working at a hair salon? Take the time to push past your first instincts for questions, because those are likely the ones that get asked all the time. Don't ask how they got into it, or if they like it. Go a little bit deeper. Ask them things like *is washing someone's hair as uncomfortably sensual for the employee as it is for the customer?* or *what happens with all the hair you cut? Are there just dumpsters full of hair out back?* The question itself doesn't have to be particularly funny, the point is to build intrigue by asking things that show that you care. By actually taking the time to think about what a person is saying you automatically make yourself more appealing to them.

To me, the perfect way to deliver an interesting question is to preface it with a funny statement. The thing about funny statements is that they are sometimes awkward to respond to. If you make a joke, there's not always a natural response for someone to make, and it discourages them from responding. If you deliver your funny statement and then immediately follow it with an interesting question you free the other person of the burden of responding to your statement. This is especially important if they don't find it particularly funny, because the desire to leave an unfunny statement on read is hard to ignore. But if they can gloss over it and be drawn back in with a question than the joke seems like more of a throwaway, and it's ok if it wasn't exactly their cup of tea.

How this works on a practical level is that you want to think of both your statement and your question before you respond at all. This makes it seem as though the thoughts are on the fly which makes them more impressive if they're good and more forgivable if they're bad. So don't even start to respond until you've thought of both. The funny statement can either be a joke about the topic or a one line funny story about something related, it's really wide open. But try to keep it as short as possible. The idea is to imply that this quick funny thought flashed in your mind, and you have to get it out before you ask the question you really wanted to ask. So you end up with something like this:

> *I love sports. I play basketball every Wednesday at the University*

> *Oh nice! I always dreamt of being in the NBA but it turns out I'm short and fat and white*

> *Are you out there dunking on kids who are just trying to get an education? What a bully!*

I shoot my shot with my joke, but then immediately move on to a question designed to get a response. By making an assertion, the other person is encouraged to respond and clear it up. And by not asking a small talk *how long have you been playing* type question I show that I'm putting a bit of thought into what they're saying. Ensuring that all of your jokes end with questions makes you keep the conversation going, which gives a better opportunity for a deeper connection.

Text Stories

When you're telling stories through text you need to be incredibly scrupulous with your editing. **The fewer words the better**. You want to get to the punchline of your story as fast as possible, because reading superfluous details is exhausting. See how annoyed you are at me for using superfluous? It's even worse through text. You want to try to make your stories as much a setup-punchline format as possible. It's ok to drop details, if it's interesting enough the other person will ask. You have to get to the meat of it all right away. Like if I have a story about going to the petting zoo with my parents when I was a kid and a couple of the goats got too close to me and knocked my hat off, and me as a kid cried and went to my mom, I need to make that story as short as possible.

Telling a story through text is almost like writing a headline for an article. You want to come up with a single sentence or two that will draw people in and have them ask questions. After all, the goal of these text conversations is to make people interested in you. So my petting zoo story could be something like: *I'm a little scared of the zoo, as a kid a gang of goats beat me up and stole my hat.* Notice I've deliberately enhanced some details and left out all of the others to make the story sound more interesting than it really is. I want the other person to be surprised and want to ask me questions. Essentially you're filling in all of the details by answering the questions which changes you telling the story from a monologue to a conversation.

Long winded stories are the absolute death of text conversations. We've all seen a wall of text come in, it's like seeing a snowstorm: you know you've got a lot of work ahead of you. Keep it as brief as you possibly can, and phrase it in such a way that it adds intrigue and encourages questions. Even the greatest storyteller isn't going to keep someone's attention through text, so do yourself a favour and edit edit edit.

Complimentary Funny

Everyone likes receiving compliments, but if they feel forced or creepy they can be uncomfortable for everyone. By working your compliments into funny statements you can make it far more organic and therefore far more impactful than a straight up compliment. It's not an easy technique to master because subtlety is of the utmost importance, but it's worth the effort. One way to do it is to challenge people on something they say was lucky by insinuating it happened because of a positive quality of theirs. If my girlfriend texted me and said something like: *I was just walking down the street and they were giving out free iced coffee samples* I would reply with something like: *Oh yeah I saw on their twitter they're doing that for hot girls, makes sense you got one.* Because it's in a joke the compliment is less awkward for the both of us. This example is not the most subtle, but I wanted to get the point across. For someone you just met, you want to downplay it a bit more than that.

I'm not going to be able to make it tonight, I got called into work.
Could we do tomorrow instead?

See this is why I like being stupid, no one ever calls me in. That's what you get for being smart. Tomorrow is fine!

Using self deprecation is a great way to compliment someone because the joke on yourself distracts from the compliment, making it seem more natural. Be careful not to rely on this too much, because if you constantly say someone is better than you, eventually they will believe it. But for frivolous things this is a great way to work it in.

Another way to slip in a compliment without it seeming too obvious is by using ironic anger. Basically when you find out a person is good at something, you become fake angry because it's unfair the advantageous they have. It looks something like this:

> *Sorry I missed your message, I was volunteering at the food bank*

> *Alright, something is fishy here. Are you a robot or an assassin or something? I refuse to believe you're this hot AND this good of a person. There's something up and I'm going to get to the bottom of it.*

The challenging energy of the message surprises the reader and helps to counteract the sappy niceness of the words. Using these tricks to obscure your compliments slightly can let you say really nice things about a person without the awkwardness of saying it directly.

Get a laugh right now
Become a compliment assassin

Turning compliments into jokes can be easy. First, come up with the direct compliment you **want** to give, then hide it a bit with a reveal.

Attractiveness:
Excuse me, could you do us all a favour and try to be a little less attractive? We're trying to work and it's very distracting.

Can you settle a bet for us? We're debating the habits of hot people - do you guys like Oreos?

Intelligence:
It's so relaxing being around smart people, no one expects me to know shit

You save me a lot of time, it's so much easier to ask you than to google. Less porn though

Niceness:
I want to understand how you can be so good to people, it's like you don't even care that they're all hot garbage!

It's inspiring how nice you are, it's like if Bob Ross had a baby with 5 nurses.

By deciding on the compliment first, you can re-word it to be less awkward and more funny.

Pictures

One of the techniques we discussed very early on in this book is the use of descriptive language to paint a funny picture for a person. Well, the upside of texting is that you can use actual pictures to get your point across. Whenever you're trying to describe how something or someone looked in a funny way, keep in mind that finding a funny picture that looks like it gets that point across instantly. It also is much clearer than any description you would give, and it's instantly recognizable. The picture doesn't have to be perfect; you can describe the slight differences in a funny way. But in a medium where you want your word count as low as possible; a quick picture will save you a thousand words.

The secret to making people like you through text is learning to blend humor with genuine messaging to show the person that you are funny, but you also care. Try not to overwhelm them with jokes but try to pick your spots. Encourage their jokes back and try to build funny moments with them. It's more difficult to gauge reactions and get a full picture of someone's humor, so start slow and use the context you have to avoid off-putting topics. By listening and empathizing with them and adding your own humor to the shared context of the conversation you'll start to notice more deeper and meaningful connections happening easier, and your matches will start to blossom into relationships.

10.2 In Person

A. Meeting Someone

Meeting someone in person seems somewhat old fashioned these days, and going out with the sole intention of finding a partner isn't nearly as important as it used to be. In fact, it's probably more difficult than ever to meet someone in the real world. However, what you'll discover is that if you become a funny person, it'll happen organically. People are drawn to funny people, so if you can emit that energy then you'll bring people to you. Connections with strangers become stronger and easier to create, and you become the kind of person people want to be with.

There are some tricks to being the kind of funny that attracts people though – we all know clowns aren't sexy. You want people to see you as confident, clever, and slightly vulnerable. It sounds easy, but it's incredibly difficult to strike that balance. It's easy to be too aggressive and come off as a bully. Or too passive to seem confident. Or even be too scared to laugh at themselves to allow for that vulnerability. And as always, it's so easy to misunderstand the context of a stranger and say things that you shouldn't.

It's about 30 nautical miles outside of the scope of this book to describe how to meet someone, but the beauty of being funny is that you can maximize every chance that you do get. By becoming funny you become someone that people are excited to show off. Friends will introduce you to more friends, and you'll notice your opportunities growing organically. So my advice below is for how to act *after* you've met someone, not how to approach a stranger and make it work. Again, this isn't about how to pick up a stranger, this is about how to make someone laugh that you're attracted to but only just met.

Like every aspect of being funny, it takes a lot of practice and honest self reflection to get right. The exact approach and details are fully dependent on your own humor, so that sense needs to be developed before being funny will help you romantically. There aren't any shortcuts, but you'll find that if you put in the work, you will revolutionize your dating life.

Relax

One of the most important things with both comedy and flirting is to not make it seem like you're trying too hard. If you're exerting a creepy amount of effort to make someone laugh or to make someone like you, it's incredibly off-putting. There's a real patheticness to it that is the antithesis of sexy, so for the love of God calm yourself down. Don't try to make a joke out of *everything*. I've said it many times before and nowhere is it more important than this: be your own toughest critic. If a joke isn't a no-doubter, don't throw it at someone you're attracted to. Save those 50/50 jokes for your friends, and only put forth your best effort. Here's the harsh truth: even if you did have an objectively great joke for everything that happens in a conversation, if you say every one of them, people will hate you.

If you try to dominate the conversation and out-funny everyone it really shows. It projects an air of insecurity, as though if you're not constantly getting the positive affirmation of laughter you'll wilt and die. It's disturbingly unattractive, so try to pick your spots.

The same goes for laughing at things that your person of interest says. You most certainly want to, but don't overdo it. A fake laugh kills sexual interest like a bad fart, so please never do that. And sometimes jokes are only meant to get a smile, so a fake laugh will be extra obvious. Be attentive and open to any jokes they make, but try to be natural.

Establish Shared Context: Personal

As much as you can, try to create shared funny moments with the person you're trying to win over. Each moment that is unique to the two of you helps build a closeness that makes them think of you fondly. Don't watch them so close that you're noticing private moments, but anything of interest that happens to them and is plainly obvious is something you want to address. We've spoken about this before, but what is different in this romantic context is that you want to be sure that you are always on their side.

What I mean by that is that you always want to be sympathetic to whatever they are feeling in the moment. If you're walking and someone bumps into them, even if they were in the wrong you want your jokes to be attacking the other person. The idea is to go beyond shared context even to create an *us against the world* sort of vibe. If the two of you can be collaboratively making fun of a target, those laughs are instrumental in create romantic feelings. Always be looking for opportunities to create these moments. It takes time to learn how to pick them out, but let's go over some examples which will illustrate what I mean.

- **Ignored:** There's nothing worse than speaking up in a group and being ignored by everyone. It cuts us right to the core. So if this person happens to find themselves in that situation and you can be there to offer a joke of condolence, it can mean a lot. The joke can be anything as long as it's clear that you've got their back. Let the moment hang long enough that it's clear no one registered the comment/question, then make sympathetic eye contact and go.

  Them: Does anyone want to go to Starbucks?
  beat
  You: I guess it's more of a Tim Horton's crowd

  The laughter comes mainly from you breaking the tension of that silence and offering your sympathies. Notice that by attacking everyone who didn't listen I'm creating that *us vs them* feel that I mentioned. It subtly builds that closeness that I'm looking for.

- **Slighted:** If the person you're trying to meet is mistreated in any way, regardless of how inconsequential, commenting on it builds a lot of likability. It shows that you are empathetic to their issues. Obviously they have noticed that they've been done wrong, and are likely thinking about it. Acknowledging it breaks that tension which leads to easy laughs and feelings of connection.

  A very easy example would be if you're out to eat in a group. Oftentimes, there will be one person receiving their food well after the others – a fact most people won't notice because they are distracted by their own food. If you can be the one person who does notice, that person will remember.

  Again, the joke doesn't have to be killer because the release of tension is the driving force here. A simple *I guess they thought you weren't hungry* is often enough to get the desired result.

- **Bothered:** When people are upset they show it in subtle ways. If you're anything like me, 99% of the time you ignore it and hope you don't have to deal with it. But if it's someone you're attracted to then acknowledging that something is wrong with them shows that you care. It's often difficult to navigate because it's awkward to ask someone you don't really know if they are alright, but sometimes it's just what they need. By asking as a joke you remove a lot of that discomfort and allow them to duck the question if they so chose. An easy way to do that is by intentionally choosing a surprising, unrealistic reason why they might be upset. *Are you ok? You look like you just heard your dog was an incel or something. Do you need me to murder someone for you?* The goal is to pick something so far off of what the real problem is that you get a laugh and then hopefully open up to you. By offering to help you're creating closeness and likeability.

This doesn't always work, and if the person looks too upset don't get involved. Ideally you want to use this for little issues that are just annoying and not actual big life issues.

- **Teased:** Even if you like being teased, striking back with a clever comeback is the most fun part. So if you notice someone being teased and you're able to come to their defence it can carry a lot of weight. This requires a bit of tact though, because you want to make sure they have a chance to respond first.
The proper way to do this is to attack the attacker, not defend the attacked. Defending is not only infinitely harder to make funny, but it is also more obvious that you're trying to suck up. Remember our section on comebacks: you want to craft a related but independently funny attack on the attacker. This makes it seem less obvious to the group that you're defending someone, but still creates the *us vs them* feel that you're going for.

There needs to be a subtlety to all of this, so it's going to take some practice. You can't make it to obvious what you're doing – the worse the jokes the more it seems like your just a suckhole. But the more shared context you can create, the closer the person feels to you.

Establish Shared Context: External

The other version of shared context that can bring you closer to a stranger is very similar to *us vs them*, except it's more of an *us against the world* approach. In this case, instead of watching your chosen person for the right moment, you want to watch the outside world for perceived danger. The implication is: *we need to watch out for each other or that thing will get us.* The idea is that there is no real danger and because there's no real danger the tension is fun and fake instead of actually worrisome.

For instance, if I was talking to a girl I had just met and some sloppy looking fellow (it's always a sloppy looking guy) walked by with one of those ridiculous over the top "I'm a tough guy" t shirts that said something like *These Colors Don't Run*, I would lean in with an ironic level of concern and say *If any trouble goes down you and I will run and hide behind that guy, they only let you buy those T-Shirts if you're a super bad ass. They make you take a test and everything.*

Even though it's clearly a joke, the *us against the world* feel subconsciously draws the two of you together. I mean, unless the person already hates you of course. But if they're into you at all it creates a closeness that is difficult to achieve as quick through any other method.

And this technique doesn't always have to be fear based. Anything that you notice out of place (spot the dog) can be twisted into an *us vs the world* sort of scenario. If you see a bag with no identifiable owner you can say something like *Alright, you go grab a cab, I'm going to grab that bag, we're going to head to the airport and start a new life with whatever is inside, deal?* A simple ironic, unexpected joke creates the illusion that we're on the lamb together. It's so simple and subtle but the more you can joke about the two of you as a team that need each other to succeed, the more that dynamic resonates in their mind.

It's not just being funny, it's being inclusively funny with a hint of intrigue that will make people romantically attracted to you.

Mull it Over
Us vs Them

Shared external context is an incredibly powerful tool for creating the feeling of closeness. The trick to exploiting it is to always be thinking about of you and the other person as *us*. Frame everything that is happening as happening to the two of you, instead of yourself.

If you see a cop, your jokes are about how they're going to catch *us*

If you see a wedding party, your jokes are about how *we* should crash it

If you walk past a mansion, your jokes are about how one day *we'll* live in it

By operating with the constant mindset of *us vs them* you not only get the benefits of shared context laughs, but you insert the thought of *us* into the audience's head, and that is the most powerful tool of all.

Don't Be Jealous

You're not the only funny person around, and often you won't even be the funniest, so don't let your ego get the better of you. If someone else is making your person of interest laugh there's a real temptation to take it as a challenge and try to prove that you're funnier. Your body will tell you to not laugh along and to try to downplay the humor of this challenger, but this is obvious to everyone.

Remember the earlier rule of *yes, and...* Instead of trying to compete with someone who is making this special person laugh, try to join with them. Tag onto their jokes and ask leading funny questions to make yourself a part of the laughter as opposed to fighting against it. People aren't automatically attracted to the funniest person around, so don't feel that is what you have to be. Instead be the person who is fun for every situation, that's the best way to deal.

Study Their Humor

Without being a creep, pay attention to what they find funny. Now that you're able to identify why things are funny you want to notice the techniques that get laughs. Do they like wordplay? Misdirection? Hyperbole? Irony? By figuring out what tricks get a response you can better jokes using those mechanisms. Obviously you should pay attention to the content of the jokes that they enjoy, but counter-intuitively the techniques themselves are often more important. If someone can't resist a surprise twist, then you know that you can go to that well to get a laugh whenever needed. There are some people who won't laugh at a pun no matter what the content is, so by studying the actual underlying mechanics of what makes someone laugh you can give yourself a huge advantage.

Let them Lead

The end goal I've set out in this book is to help you understand all of the building blocks of humor, and then be able to use those to create funny. Once you've practiced up enough you will start to realize that with these tools you can make essentially *anything* funny. And this is never more useful then when flirting with a stranger. The way to really impress someone with humor is to be able to get a laugh using whatever they are saying.

It starts by having the broad knowledge base that I talked about earlier, but even with very minimal knowledge you can make a joke about any topic. The point is that you don't want to force a subject simply because you have jokes about it, you want to take what they're giving you and make it funny. Resist the urge to start a funny story out of nowhere, or force a funny idea where it doesn't belong. Save that for your friends. In this case, you want them to lead – either through statements or questions.

It helps immensely to have prepared stories/answers for questions that you get a lot. *What do you do? Do you live around here? What do you do for fun?* It seems like it's cheating to prepare answers, but it makes a huge difference. Sure, you can make funny out of nothing, but help yourself out when you can. Have a funny story about your job and your neighbourhood and your apartment. You want it to be at your fingertips when it's brought up, as opposed to finding a way to wedge it in yourself. That way it feels much more organic.
The more you can flow with the conversation and add funny to the topics that other people bring up, the more naturally funny you will feel. If you have a great story or a fantastic insight to some topical event, wait for it to come up naturally. Don't force it in yourself. If you do that with all your best ideas you'll find yourself burning out too quickly in an interaction. Also, jokes on the current topic of discussion benefit from the boost of existing context so people are more open to the idea. The more funny with the flow you can be, the more people are going to find you irresistible.

B. Dating

Whether through dating apps or meeting someone in person, the goal is usually to start dating. Maybe you're just trying to bang for now, but *eventually* you're going to look to hang out with someone consistently. Hopefully it's someone that both makes you laugh and appreciates your humor, but to keep it that way you have to grow and evolve. The first few weeks of dating are incredibly important since that's where most relationships flounder.

The *getting to know you* stage is where you set the foundation for who you are in this relationship. This might be overselling it a bit, but it's a chance for you to reinvent yourself. This person knows very little about you so whatever you present is what you've always been to them. And what that means for us is that if you walk into this new relationship as a confidently funny person, even if you haven't been that in the past, to them it's as though you always were. Building your confidence through humor in other areas allows you to be more confident in your relationships.

As you spend time with this person, be extra vigilant in observing and learning what they find funny. You know yourself the feeling of someone who completely understands your sense of humor – it feels like the completely understand you as a person. You can be that person for whoever you're seeing! Because the beautiful thing about understanding how funny works is that you can appreciate all kinds of humor. So if you like this person, you can appreciate and understand their sense of humor, even if it isn't perfectly aligned with yours.
I know my partner's sense of humor so well that I can spot the smallest thing that I know she'll find especially funny. Whether it be an article, a picture, or even a gif and I'll share that with her, and she does the same. Simple acts like that are a great display that you understand someone, and that is incredibly attractive to people.

It takes time, so don't think that you understand them more than you do. Really listen and empathize and try to understand their context and then use this to make them laugh. It's not just being funny that attracts people to you, it's being funny in an empathetic way that shows your beliefs align with theirs. The more you can understand this the more you can be the kind of funny that makes people want to be with you.

Every person and every relationship is different, so there are no clear-cut approaches that work in every situation. But there are some huge mistakes that I've seen people make that can really tank a relationship, and by people I mean myself. Here are some practical tips that you can use on top of what we've already learned.

Watch your negativity

A lot of comedy comes from attacking things, but if that is all you do you run the risk of becoming a drain on people. It's easy to tear things down so I often get caught in a pattern of trying to smash everything, but it's incredibly frustrating for the audience. If every time they broach a topic or idea all you do is shoot it down they become discouraged from talking to you. People don't want to be around that kind of energy. Even if the target is yourself, it will start to wear on people. You have to make a concerted effort to be positive often enough to balance out your negativity.

It's harder to spot things out of place when they're good, because joy doesn't really breed comedy the way tragedy does. But do it. If it's an extra beautiful day, make a joke about that. *Did you drug me and take me to Florida or something? It's suspiciously nice out.* If your partner put in the effort to look special, make a positive joke about that *Oh shit I didn't know I ordered the **extra** hot today.* By keeping a balance between your positive and negative observations you keep things from becoming stale.

Train your Brain
Un-negative your negativity

My default humor is to tear something down. I enjoy it. I find it cathartic. But over the years, my partners have let me know how draining it is. So now, when I'm primed for some real complaining humor, I try to spin it to sound more positive. In this exercise, you're going to take negative jokes and give them a more positive spin.

Example:
It's too goddam hot out, I feel like a fat stupid rotisserie chicken

More positive:
This heat is more convenient than working out, I'm sweating off an obese toddler's worth of weight a day

Now you try:

1) *This show sucks so much I might use it to vacuum my living room*
2) *I hate this guy with the same passion the pope hates a woman's right to choose*
3) *I hope the idiot who thought one bus an hour is enough gets anal fissures*

Limiting your negativity is crucial for being funny in relationships, so keep that positive attitude.

Never belittle

There is a subtle but hugely important difference between a tease and an insult, and learning that is paramount to understanding sustained flirting. The tricky thing is that the determining factor is the victim of the joke, so understanding their context is vital. A tease is akin to a tickle – it's discomfort meant to illicit laughter. And like tickling some people don't like it, and for everyone, too much is agony. An insult on the other hand is more biting than it is funny, and the implication is that there is something lacking in the person.

The difference is hard to explain but easy to notice. For instance, if I was walking along in front of a group of people and then slipped and fell into the pool, my girlfriend would want to joke about it later. The difference between her teasing me and her insulting me is that the tease implies I was the victim of circumstance, whereas the insult implies I'm an idiot who deserved it.

Tease: *You had that panicked look on your face like a cat who accidentally fell in the tub.*
Insult: *Captain Balance over here hasn't even learned how to walk yet*

In the tease it's the world's fault, whereas the insult implies it's your fault. It's a small thing but it changes the feel from laughing at the person to laughing with them. *Us vs the world* is just as applicable in dating as it is in meeting someone. You want that person to view you as a team, so the more you treat it that way the better. Never insult, and if you're worried that your tease may have been taken as an insult, apologize immediately.

Ask Questions

When we're hanging out with someone we like, we want to make them laugh as much as possible. And without noticing we can sometimes end up dominating the conversation talking about ourselves. Because we have so many funny stories and thoughts and we just want to share them. But you're being an asshole. Ask the person questions about themselves. Interesting questions. Listen and actually care about the topics. Don't make the questions the jokes but use them to tease out more information that you can then make jokes about together.

Be confident in your ability to find the funny in whatever they are talking about and resist the urge to dominate the conversation. Wait for them to ask you and then have your funny story ready instead of shoehorning it in where it doesn't belong. The more you can learn about the other person the more you can understand their context and their humor and use it to build a funny, meaningful relationship.

Respect their opinions

When your partner tells you something in earnest, respect that and don't make fun. It's similar to belittling; you want to create a team atmosphere. And to do that is to respect their likes and opinions. Resist the urge to make fun and instead ask questions and find interesting aspects of what their saying. Make fun of your preconceived notions of the idea instead of the idea itself, that way you're attacking the prejudices against the idea and you're on the same team.

If your partner confesses that they're into video games but you hate them, don't call them a loser. Even if they are a loser. Ask them to explain what they enjoy about them and make fun of your preconceived notions. *I always thought games were for losers but that sounds cool as shit, I guess I'm the loser.* By making it feel as though they've won you over to their idea/hobby/activity you show that you respect them and listen to them and that goes such a long way.

Callback to their jokes

One of the main things I've tried to impart in this book is that laughing with other people is a great way to make them feel as though you're funny. The next level to that is to actually remember their jokes and tell them back to them. It's a very cheap and easy way for you to both relive a laugh and to make the person feel good about themselves, which in turn makes them more attracted to you. *I watched the Matrix the other day and I couldn't stop thinking about when you called that big fat guy in the leather coat **Amorpheous**. It was so funny it ruined the movie.* If you're re-laughing at a joke they told it's guaranteed to incite new laughter.

These are just a few examples, but the idea is that you need to empathize with your partner as much as possible. Learn what makes them laugh – both techniques and content – and use the tools from this book to exploit them. Try to create and *us vs them* feel and be positive and complimentary. The goal is to create a dynamic where it's always you two laughing at something, even if it's yourself. Anytime you're laughing and they aren't you're doing something wrong. People are so caught up thinking that being funny is all about them, but with relationships more than anything else, you need to focus on the other person.

It's undeniable that a good sense of humor is an unbeatable tool to establish and maintain a relationship, but just being funny isn't enough. By practicing the techniques I've shown you here and working on your empathy you will find your connections becoming deeper and more meaningful. By learning to appreciate and align with someone's sense of humor you can show them that you not only understand what makes them laugh, but you also understand them as a person. And in the end, that's what we're all looking for.

Epilogue

Being funny is far and away the most powerful driver of success in my life – it's given me everything I have. It's taken me around the world, given me friends in every city, and made me never want for romantic companionship. In no way should you expect those things. I've dedicated my life to understanding funny and likely you are just starting your journey. The analogy of working out holds true here, you wouldn't expect to be a professional athlete on your first session. In fact, if you go into it with that attitude, you'll never make it. Becoming funny is like getting in shape: you learn the basics, start to apply them, and with consistent effort you start to see amazing results. When you see someone in unbelievable shape you know they didn't start like that. It's years of work. When you see someone funny it's the same thing. Whether conscious or unconscious, they've spent hours and hours of time working on becoming funny. There's no shortcut.

That said, the techniques and tips in this book are a start along the way. They are meant to help your mind start to think about what is funny. They are tools to deconstruct what you laugh at and learn to build those things yourself. But it's what you do with those tools that matters. If you take what I've shown you and apply it and work it and mould it to fit your specific personality, I guarantee you'll notice an uptick in all areas of your life. Most importantly being funny is a way to build confidence, just like working out. The more laughs you get, the better you'll feel about yourself. Almost ever funny person became funny to overcome something, and they'll all tell you how much it helped them. It can do the same for you.

Start by mimicking things that make you laugh. Change them slightly to fit your personality but try them on. Get that feeling of laughter. Really think about why those things are funny and what is making people laugh. Get comfortable, and then apply those same ideals to your own thoughts. Be free with your thoughts but careful with your words. Always remember context should drive your content, and expectation should guide your wording. You want the joke to consist of material that is pleasant to the audience phrased in a way that will delight them.

Don't get discouraged if a joke bombs, it happens all the time. But do learn from it. Really sit down and think about what it was that didn't get across the way you meant it. It's usually missing context or lack of surprise in your reveal. Be honest with yourself. The natural reaction is to blame the audience, we professionals do it all the time. But if we're honest, we're usually the problem. Chances are good that you're not giving enough context, or you're missing some key information. If a joke doesn't get a laugh but you're sure it's funny, re-word it and try it on someone else. The only way to learn is to fail, and it hurts, but if you can be truthful with yourself you won't fail for long.

And remember that the main goal is to have fun. We've focused entirely on making other people laugh, but a bonus of understanding funny is that you can make yourself laugh. Once being funny is second nature, you'll start to notice that funny thoughts appear seemingly out of nowhere. Your brain is so wired to think funny that it can spot the dog before you know it and surprise yourself. Learning to be funny is a gift that you can give yourself, and it benefits everyone around you.

Good luck and keep laughing.